"Most people with mental disorders do not receive any mental health treatment. Those who seek out psychotherapy do so because they believe that such services will be helpful. Unfortunately, many suffering individuals fail to be engaged in psychotherapy and dropout early in treatment (most after the first session)—before they had the opportunity to benefit fully. What are we doing wrong?

Daryl Chow, in this engaging book, shows us what we have been doing wrong and more importantly, what we should be doing differently. Throw out the traditional assessment of psychopathology and engage the client with the fervor that is necessary to form an alliance that provides the scaffolding for therapy to work. From the very first minute, focus on the client and their suffering and don't hide behind the sterile clinical approach of traditional history taking and clinical diagnoses. This book walks the talk—you will be engaged from the very first moment of picking up the book!"

—**Bruce E. Wampold, Ph.D.**,
author of the Great Psychotherapy Debate; Director, Research Institute, Modum Bad Psychiatric Center; Professor Emeritus, University of Wisconsin.

D1521509

"Author Daryl Chow is a leading researcher on using Deliberate Practice to improve clinical effectiveness. In this book, he provides practical guidance on one of the most important and challenging moments in therapy: your first encounter with your clients. Clearly organized in sequential steps, Daryl Chow shows us how to get past the sacred but ineffective "intake session" and instead discover how to truly connect with our clients. The text is research-based as well as grounded in his honest and courageous self-disclosure.

This book is highly recommended for all therapists, from trainees to experienced clinicians who want to improve their effectiveness."

— Tony Rousmaniere, PsyD, author of Deliberate Practice for Psychotherapists.

"An elegantly written book of practical wisdom, humour and loads of humanity—one that you would go back to every now and then, regardless of level of practice. Daryl shares selflessly, what it means to add life to the life of another in therapy."

–Juliana Toh, M.Sc. (Family & Systemic Psychotherapy), Clinical Director of Counselling and Care Centre, Singapore.

"Daryl Chow has finally written The Book I've wanted every therapist to read for years. The First Kiss reminds all of us--from students to seasoned veterans—that the first imperative of our work is to hear and understand the people who seek our services —in their terms. With an ease and generosity that make the reader feel like they're chatting over coffee with Daryl rather than reading words on a page, Dr. Chow welcomes us into his world as a creative and erudite scholar-practitioner. Once there, we experience what becomes possible when we become relationally responsive to people rather than rigidly robotic with intake procedures. This book should become dog-eared, papered with post-its, and full of multi-colored highlighting."

"Thoroughly engaging and enjoyable read! Daryl writes in such a personable way, much like him. A highly recommended book, for both learners and seasoned practitioners. *The First Kiss* brings into sharp focus that scared space between the client and the therapist, and how to continuously shape and co-construct this space, even after the first session."
—Neo Eng Chuan, MA (Psych),
Principal Psychologist & Founder, CaperSpring, Singapore.

"Daryl Chow has delivered a majestic, digestible, and real approach to psychotherapy. He blends current research with his clinical wisdom in a way that is approachable and practical. His honesty, humility, and humor make this work a must read for any psychotherapist."
—Jesse Owen, Ph.D.,
Associate Professor & Department Chair, Department of Counseling Psychology at the University of Denver.

"Exactly as anticipated, Daryl Chow goes above and beyond expectations. At a time when few therapists have time to read as much as they would like, Chow's latest offering is as accessible as it is indispensable. Open this book to any page and you will become inspired."
—David S. Prescott,
Senior Associate, International Center for Clinical Excellence, Co-Editor, Feedback-Informed Treatment in Clinical Practice: Reaching for Excellence.

"Fun, accessible, and practical—words rarely used to describe the writings of a researcher! But Daryl Chow is more than a researcher, he's a skilled clinician with a passion to change the field of psychotherapy. In his book, "The First Kiss," Daryl invites readers to consider how an approach based on engagement—beginning with intake and the first few sessions—serves as a vehicle for creating greater impact, and ultimately, better therapy outcomes. "The First Kiss" is a brilliant dance between research and practice, with Daryl's transparency providing readers with opportunities to hear, see, and think differently about psychotherapy. Through anecdotes and stories from a myriad of fields, case illustrations, and yes, practical examples real-world examples, "The First Kiss" accomplishes something that few books of this kind do—it keeps the reader "engaged" from beginning to end. I highly recommend this book!"

–Bob Bertolino, Ph.D.,
Professor of Rehabilitation Counseling, Maryville University and Sr. Clinical Advisor at Youth In Need, Inc. Author of Effective Counseling and Psychotherapy: An Evidence-Based Approach

"With elegant simplicity and intelligence, practitioner, trainer and researcher Daryl Chow guides the field of mental health in the right direction. In this much needed book, The First Kiss confronts the hard facts of what the research evidence tells us about what works in psychotherapy, and gives us a clear and concise description on how to become better practitioners. Follow his lead and you will achieve better results with higher quality in less time."

–Birgit Villa, Psychologist, author of "Videre – Hvordan psykiske helsetjenester kan bli bedre" ("Further – How Mental Health Services Can Be Better") and Director of a Mental Health Service, Norway.

"This book speaks to a holistic approach to psychotherapeutic practice that guides the first session as well as addressing what should be in every therapy session. Daryl Chow is a thought leader because he realises that in this day and age of accountability, quality assurance and continuous improvement expectations from funders as well as the community that we have to improve our outcomes for clients. We have to improve our

game. He is a pragmatist who knows that sometimes you only get one session to make a difference with a client. This is an accessible book that shares lots of practical examples and suggestions that apply equally to the experienced therapist or novice. It will be prescribed reading for my supervisees!"
–Kaye Frankcom,
Clinical & Counselling Psychologist, ICCE accredited trainer,
Melbourne, Australia.

"Good psychotherapy should be an engaging experience, but the question is how can we therapists create meaningful life-changing moments? This book highlights where we tend to go wrong in psychotherapy and how we can make a much deeper connection with our clients about what matters most to them. In each concise chapter, Daryl offers valuable reflections and useful tools, to improve the way you engage in psychotherapy."
–Ben Mullings, Ph.D. (Counselling Psychologist),
Director of Likeminds Clinic,
Leader of the Australian Mental Health Party.

THE FIRST KISS

Undoing the Intake Model and Igniting First Sessions in Psychotherapy

By

Daryl Chow, MA, Ph.D. (Psych)

The moral right of the author has been asserted.
Cover design by Emma Hardy.
Author photo by Jeremiah Ang.

ISBN-13: 978-0-6482670-1-0
Ebook ISBN: 978-0-6482670-0-3

VISIT: darylchow.com/firstkiss

Correlate
PRESS

Dedicated to

Fr. Claude Barreteau, *MEP (1929-2011)*

When I had no words in our first conversation,
you sat with me in silence.

ABOUT THE AUTHOR

Daryl Chow, MA, Ph.D. (Psych) is a practicing psychologist and trainer. He is a senior associate of the International Center for Clinical Excellence (ICCE). He devotes his time to workshops, consultations and researches on the development of expertise and highly effective psychotherapists, helping practitioners to accelerate learning and improve client outcomes.

Based on his doctoral research on the role of deliberate practice in cultivating superior performance in psychotherapy, Daryl and colleagues' 2015 peer-reviewed article was nominated the "Most Valuable Paper" by the American Psychological Association (APA). His work is featured in two chapters of two edited books in 2017, *Cycle of Excellence: Using Deliberate Practice to Improve Supervision and Training*, and Feedback-Informed Treatment in Clinical Practice: Reaching for Excellence. He is the author of several articles, a contributor to edited books, and the co-editor of *The Write to Recovery: Personal Stories & Lessons about Recovery from Mental Health Concerns*.

Daryl's blog, Frontiers of Psychotherapist Development (darylchow.com/frontiers) is aimed at inspiring and sustaining practitioner's individualised professional development.

Currently, Daryl maintains a private practice with a vibrant team at Henry Street Centre, Fremantle, and continues to serve as a senior psychologist at the Institute of Mental Health, Singapore. In a previous life, he was a youth worker. He lives in Western Australia with his wife and two kids. He continues to obsess about the craft of psychotherapy and music.

For more information, visit darylchow.com

CONTENTS

LEAN BACK: A FOREWORD

Doing therapy is not an activity that came naturally to me. As we watched videos of master clinicians, many of my fellow classmates quickly understood, and were able to identify, both what was happening and would transpire next. I, by contrast, struggled, often finding myself lost in the content and uncertain about what to do to help.

I desperately wanted to learn. Leaning in to the task, I read every article and book my professors assigned, and then some. Throughout my graduate years, I volunteered for two local professional organizations. In exchange for pasting mailing labels to workshop brochures and serving coffee at their events, I was grated free admission to scores of trainings with nationally recognized experts. In 1985, I even traveled to Phoenix, Arizona to work as a volunteer at the first *Evolution of Psychotherapy* conference. Although I was loath to admit it, I left feeling more bewildered than ever.

I vowed to work harder.

Four years later, I took a position at the Brief Family Therapy

Center (BFTC) in Milwaukee, Wisconsin. I'd met Insoo Berg—one-half of the brain trust at that clinic—at one of the continuing educations workshops I'd attended during graduate school. Why she eventually offered me a job, I will never know. What I can say for certain is that it was *not* because—despite my having read everything she and her partner Steve de Shazer had ever written —I understood psychotherapy!

One day, not long after my arrival, I was scheduled to meet with a client. Steve, Insoo, and several other clinicians, were seated in an adjoining room, behind a one-way mirror. This was the way we worked. Every session was observed live. A phone connected to the rooms, allowing the two sides to communicate if necessary. Additionally, a short break just before the end of each visit gave the client a moment to reflect on the hour, and the team and therapist a chance to consult. Usually, a summary and suggestions followed.

It wasn't long before the phone buzzed on the table beside my chair. Picking up the handset, Steve whispered softly, yet firmly in my ear, "Lean back in your chair." It was both interesting and unexpected advice. And while I wasn't exactly sure why I should, I instantly did as I'd been told. The session resumed.

Not much time elapsed before the phone signaled again. Coming so soon after the last call in, it was a bit jarring. Steve was once again on the line. This time, his tone was slightly sterner.

"Sit back in the damn chair," he said and abruptly hung up.

Although startled, I did as instructed, scooching bit by bit until my butt was firmly planted at the back of the chair, all the while carrying on the conversation with my client.

On hearing the buzzing a third time, I instantly noticed where I was sitting. Somehow, I was once again perched at the edge of my seat, *leaning forward* toward the client. How, I wondered, had this happened?

"If you don't sit back in your chair," Steve said loudly, "I'm going to come in there and duct tape your back to the seat!"

I leaned back in my chair, this time for good. In the process, I learned something valuable about myself and psychotherapy. I was, and had been, so intent on doing a good job, I ended up focusing more on me—what I knew or did not know, what questions I should or shouldn't ask, or interventions might be best—than on the person I was there to help. Steve's advice was simple and direct: *stop trying to figure out what to say or do next*. Instead, "Lean back in your chair." In short, listen.

When I read *The First Kiss,* I was instantly reminded of my experience with Steve at the BFTC. The principles this slim volume offers are both simple and direct. "Any intelligent fool," Albert Einstein once observed, "can make things bigger, more complex." The field (and certainly my personal experience) attest to this fact. "It takes a touch of genius," Einstein continued, "and a lot of courage, to move in the opposite direction." As you will soon experience for yourself, Daryl Chow has chosen the latter.

My advice?

Lean back in your chair and turn the page.

Scott D. Miller, Ph.D.
April 16th, 2018
Chicago, IL (USA)
scottdmiller.com

The First Kiss

UNDOING THE INTAKE MODEL AND IGNITING FIRST SESSIONS IN PSYCHOTHERAPY

1 **BREAKING THE SACRED RULES**

Take less, Give more.

Undo the Intake Model; make engagement sacred.

2 **INCREASING YOUR IMPACT**

Define Your Client's Circle of Development.

Work on improving the process that is influenceable and predictive of outcomes.

Create an impactful emotional memory of the first session.

3 **BUILDING A CULTURE OF LEARNING**

Build a culture of learning, and not just performing.

Cultivate this from the first session, in order to influence the entire process of therapy.

INTRODUCTION

Don't study the end result. Study the first step.

~ Josh Shipp

I grew up as a shy and anxious kid. Though most people see me as a relatively calm person, for the first ten years of clinical practice as a psychologist, right before a first session, I'd get a sick feeling in my stomach. Often, I'd get the runs in the morning. It was a real struggle. The nervousness was as bad as going on a first date. Unlike the low headcount I had in the dating scene, I had to deal with a lot more encounters with new clients, sometimes seeing four to six new clients in a week, on top of an existing heavy caseload. The anxiety was unrelenting.

For the most part, I was working in a mental health institution and hospital settings. I oscillated between two approaches to manage the nerves of first sessions. I either devoured all the person's past medical records (patients in our hospital were usually seen by a psychiatrist before being referred to us), or I avoided the case files like the plague. For the latter, I reasoned with myself that by doing so I was curtailing biases since the case notes were diagnostic-laden descriptions. Both approaches worked for a while but failed eventually because ultimately, they didn't address the real problem I was quietly confronting:

How do I engage a person in the first session?

The reason this was a challenge was that I was at odds with the way I was trained. In the traditional pedagogy, I was taught to conduct a thorough clinical assessment. Early in my career, working in a private psychiatric ward, we used to conduct a free intake assessment for outpatients. It was a marketing device. Its purpose was to lure people into our services. That's not to say it wasn't effective in helping some people take the first step. This helped many make sense of their problems and engender hope that it could be dealt with by our services. But what I was struggling with was the people who didn't come back after the free intake assessment. Whatever happened to them? Did they get the help that they needed?

When I moved to work in a large national mental health institution, though there was no "free intake assessment" ploy, the problem was the same. We would run an intake assessment, before the "real" therapy began.

There's a saying that doubt is a good servant and a bad master. For more than a decade, self-doubt had been my master, and I was the servant. I was plagued by clients dropping out before experiencing any benefit. Because I've been systematically collecting outcome data[1] early in my career, I began to dig up the dirt. As I analysed my outcomes, I noticed that there were a bunch of folks who came for a first visit and then went off the radar. In fact, I couldn't even recall who many of them were!

Here's what I found in my outcomes: In the first three years working in the mental health institution in Singapore, even though my average number of sessions was seven, my mode number of sessions (in statistical terms, mode simply means the most frequent number that appears in the data) was two. This meant that many people were coming for two sessions and then discontinue treatment. This is not to say that number of sessions is the primary metric to look out for. The main aim we should strive for is **client benefit**. But it's hard to aim for improvement of client well-being if they aren't returning for therapy!

Then I discovered something small, but significant. I was not alone in this issue of premature termination. This hidden fact only struck me later in my profession when I began consulting with agencies who were invested in improving their service deliveries and professional development for their staffs. When I looked at their raw outcome data, I noticed that even though most teams have average performance, and also have clients attend an average of four to six sessions (similar to existing research), an often undetected piece of data is that **a large percentage of clients attended only ONE session**. In my naivety, I was shocked at first. I shared this with the agencies. Many of the practitioners and their management were scratching their heads, given that they were using outcome management systems and had their eyes on the data. It wasn't their fault. The problem was this: Clients who attended one session only were removed from the dataset, therefore, not on their radar.

This disturbed me. I dug up a study that my colleague Sharon Lu and I conducted in 2009, which examined the impact of employing feedback measures to aid clinicians in an outpatient setting. I reanalysed the data, and this time to no surprise, the same finding emerged. For every hundred clients that are seen, nearly 30 in our business as usual group attended only one session and did not return for subsequent sessions.[2]

Then I came across one of Michael Yapko's training, and he mentioned the same statistic in the United States — the most frequent number of sessions attended was one. In the United Kingdom, a national audit called Improving Access to Psychological Therapies (IAPT) programme found that while the recovery rates were close to national benchmarks of 50%, this analysis did not include clients who did not attend more than one session. In fact, out of 32,382 clients, 10,500 (32%) of them had "no evidence" of more than one session.[3]

I got obsessed; I dug a little deeper. It turned out that one of the first reviews of premature termination in psychotherapy, conducted in 1975, indicated that 20 to 57% of clients drop out of treatment after the first session.[4] A more recent study in 2008 estimated that 32% terminated therapy after the first session.[5] (A coincidence that the same percentage was reported in the IAPT study mentioned earlier).

A pattern was emerging. So I went back and reanalysed my own outcomes. Somehow, over the next three years in the same setting in Singapore, my average number of sessions was six, but now the majority of clients attended four sessions; an increase of two sessions. When I moved to Australia and worked in a group private practice, my average number of sessions moved to 8.42, and my mode number of sessions increased to eight. The truth was I had no idea at that time what I was doing differently that improved the sustained engagement of the majority of my clients.

This book is my attempt to deconstruct what happened and what I've learned along the way.

It took me several months to reconcile the differences of my first sessions with practitioners in agencies that I was consulting with, as well as determine the cause of my increase in engagement across time. I was sure I wasn't unique in my ability of retaining clients for more than one session. As I spoke with more practitioners about this, the overarching problem in our field became apparent:

The way we were trained to conduct a clinical intake assessment does not engage clients.

I recalled one therapist telling me about his attempts to run the full Minnesota Multiphasic Personality Inventory (MMPI) at the intake session, so that he can get a good profile of the person. If you're familiar with the MMPI, you know it can take anything from two to three hours to complete. What is the point of getting a thorough profile of your client if they are not going to continue to work through their struggles in therapy? Clinical curiosity should not be at the client's expense.

Unplanned termination of therapy after the first session is a problem for both sides. From the client's perspective, they not only take the steps to make time, effort and money to work on their concerns, but they also have to break through feelings of vulnerability about revealing one's inner-life to a perfect stranger. From the mental health service provider's perspective, we've lost a client. We've dropped the ball. It's not even about the money, but It's like a customer entering a home-improvement store, ready to buy a particular piece of equipment, only to walk out empty-handed because you didn't provide proper guidance in the sea of options.

Some practitioners might raise the people-just-want-fast-food argument, therefore people don't sustain through the course of therapy. Professor Robert Cialdini offers a useful example of restaurants. He says that restaurants do better when they give their customers something to eat (e.g., yohurt) when they are waiting in line. "Economists say 'Don't give them food.' Psychologists say, 'Give them food because you'd give them what they need.'"[6] While it sounds counterintuitive giving customers something to eat for free while they are waiting, reducing their hunger pangs fosters a higher satisfaction and pleasurable dining experience. Giving customers a "pre-entree" is not the same as serving them "fast food". It engages the person.

Instead of just "taking" information, we need to give our clients something to hold on to in the first session as well.

My outcomes data alone wasn't helping to provide a better understanding of the problem at hand. I began to re-examine my video recordings of my first sessions (see the chapter Recording Your First Sessions). How did I subconsciously unschooled myself from a typical intake assessment?

It became apparent when I compared my recordings with my supervisees' recordings of their first sessions. It dawned on me that the way I ran first sessions was exactly the opposite of what I was taught to do. Somehow, I deviated from the traditional script. Instead, I pursued a path to find a way to amplify and magnetise each person in therapy so that they would feel the pull to want to work through the distress that brought them to see me.

Thanks to the many wonderful mentors and teachers I've met on my journey, I was able to unhook myself from the notion of particular ways of doing therapy. I had to find my own way. I believe we all have to find our own way.

This short book is a cumulation of some trials and many errors. It is an unabashing "how-to" book, based on key principles of engagement. I'm not suggesting that this is "the way." I'm aware that I'm somewhat playful in my engagement style, and I generally eschew sticking to a particular treatment modality. That said, I generally think in systemic terms, and aspire to make sessions more experiential.

I wrote this book for two reasons. First, I wrote this to clarify what I think I know. As I do that, I'm trying to weed out stuff that isn't necessary in a first session. Ask any filmmaker and they will tell you that the role of an editor is a crucial one. They take reels of footage, splice and sequence them in a way that creates an impactful scene. I strive to do this as I write. Many initial ideas for this book didn't make the cut.

Second, my aim for this book is to provide an alternative voice. I'm aware that many books on the first session in psychotherapy exist. If you want something more comprehensive on dealing with dropouts, I highly recommend you check out Joshua Swift and Roger Greenberg's (2015) excellent book, *Premature Termination in Psychotherapy*. On the topic of first sessions, I recommend Robert Tabibi's (2016) *The Art of The First Session*. It's more thorough than this book. My only credential for this book is that I offer a different perspective. As you will notice, I've grafted many ideas outside the world of psychotherapy.

Based on 13 years of collecting my outcomes data for every session, I've somehow managed to improve my engagement levels with clients.

I hope when practitioners read this book, they either apply some of these principles in their own fashion, or come to disagree with the ideas. Please, honor any dissenting voice in you. For example, some might still vehemently swear by conducting a thorough assessment before beginning any formal treatment process. If so, I love to hear from you. (Remember, I'm a student, and I don't claim to be a pre-ordained master therapist).

I invite you to use this book as a guide, like one of those daily meditation books. Recommended dose: Read one short chapter per day. For the slightly more enthusiastic and impatient, no one's going to stop you from reading it all at one go. And you can, simply because this book is written in a way that doesn't harp on a point for too long. And just to be clear, you will not be able to apply every single idea to your first sessions. Treat this book like a buffet.

The stuff that you will see in **Section I: Breaking the Sacred Rules** will give you a different lens to look through. **Section II: Increasing Your Impact** will offer you practical ways to increase the level of impact you create in the first session with your clients. **Section III: Building a Culture of Development** will help you develop a strong foundation and a scaffold for your ongoing professional development, especially in the way you conduct your first sessions. Use them to sharpen your view, not as a dogma to adhere by.

Certainly, these aren't the only core principles of how to conduct a good first therapy session. But these stood out for me. I am not offering another model of therapy—I am **not interested in creating new methods, but in developing principles.** I serve them here as heuristics, or even shortcuts. Author Nassim Taleb calls them "rules of thumb". In other words, these rules of thumb are rough and quick guides. Don't mistake them for the road. Treat them like signposts on your journey.

David Foster Wallace said that good nonfiction was a chance to "watch somebody reasonably bright but also reasonably average pay far closer attention and think at far more length about all sorts of different stuff than most of us have a chance to in our daily lives."[7]

Borrowing from chess prodigy turned martial arts expert, Joshua Waitzkin, this book is about "working on the micro to get at the macro." In other words, one of the key ways to learn is to shine our magnifying glass on specific aspects of the clinical work, deconstruct it, study it, and find ways to make the first session count, like your first kiss.

Let's begin.

SECTION I: BREAKING THE SACRED RULES

Take less, Give more.

Undo the Intake Model; make engagement sacred.

INTRODUCTION TO BREAKING
THE SACRED RULES

I will contrast the traditional Intake Model typically employed in the first sessions of psychotherapy with a personal Engagement Model. We will begin to unpack some of the reasons clients disengage early in the treatment process, why we should focus less on conducting an Intake, and prioritise what clients are *receiving* in the first session.

The contrast between the Intake Model and the Engagement Model is not to beat down a straw man. Rather, the intention is for an immediate course correction.

1. INTAKE SECOND (NOT FIRST)

The Intake Model tells us to conduct a thorough clinical assessment before we begin to "intervene". We were taught to find out as much about a client's presenting problem, their family background, psychiatric history, etc. As logical as the Intake Model may seem, when the first session is oriented towards only getting information about our client, we lose our clients in the first session. Your client leaves feeling unhelped.

I propose a different perspective. An Engagement Model.[1]

Simply stated, an Engagement Model focuses on the degree the client actively participates in the treatment process. In order for this to happen, we first need to create a climate of emotional safety. This is vital to promoting a holding environment that facilitates growth and igniting hope in our clients from the first session. An Engagement Model says that while it is necessary to know our clients first, it is not necessary to know *everything* about our client. In fact, we may even have some background information missing at the end of the first session. An Engagement Model prescribes that assessment and interventions are ongoing. A good first session is more about what you suspend doing, than what you actually did.

While the Intake Model values information, the Engagement Model prioritises connection.

The former is interested in what information the therapist needs, and the latter focuses on what the client needs. The Engagement Model sees that one of the most important things in the first session is to lay the groundwork that facilitates deep engagement,[2] and not over-emphasise getting a thorough intake.

An Engagement Model holds dear the lingering questions in our client's mind: "*Can you relate? Can you appreciate the depths of my suffering? Do you understand me at a deep level?*" As Carl Rogers says, "when a person realizes he has been deeply heard, his eyes moisten. I think in some real sense he is weeping for joy. It is as though he were saying, 'Thank God, somebody heard me. Someone knows what it's like to be me.'"[3]

For clients to be seen earlier by a therapist, an agency decided to employ a triage officer. Based on an Intake Model, this meant that they would dedicate a trainee psychologist to conduct an intake session, and then farm the client out to a psychologist to conduct the therapy. By the way, the client would also have to pay a full fee for the intake interview, making the finance department rather pleased with this new process. This is a broken system. It might look sensible from a macro perspective, but makes no sense if you were the person in need of help.[4]

We are taught to begin with the end in mind. We should still think ahead. However, it would be a detriment to believe that, "Once we've conducted a good psychological assessment and create a good case formulation, we can work through the many layers of the psyche and get to the core stuff." If we fail to engage in the first session, our client might not see a future working with us.

Begin with the *beginning* in mind. Keep first things first. This helps to keep the first session focused.

See also 2. **The Perils of an Intake Model**, 6. **Remove the Gatekeeper.**

2. THE PERILS OF AN INTAKE MODEL

The average number of sessions for an agency is about four to six.[1]

And if you've read the introduction, you'd know that the most frequent number of sessions attended by clients is **one**.[2]

What does this mean? First, averages can be deceiving. Statistician and essayist Nassim Taleb gives a useful example: "Say your average daily water consumption needs to be one liter a day and I gave you ten liters one day and none for the remaining nine days, for an average of one liter a day. Odds are you won't survive... Someone who tells you 'I drank one liter of water per day *on average*' is not conveying much information at all; there needs to be a second dimension, the variations around such an average."[3]

We may be inclined to say that the client may have benefited from the single session and did not see a need to return. This may be possible. But can you see how this sort of self-explanation strips us from any sense of agency? Evidence suggests that when clients experience some initial benefit, they are more likely to return for treatment. Besides, we cannot be of further help to someone if they do not show up!

Second, premature termination is a huge cost to the system. Perhaps the biggest unquantifiable cost may be demoralisation of the client who came and left without feeling helped.

Imagine if you are in a difficult place in your life. You broke through the shame attached to seeking help, and set aside some time and money to see a professional. You arrive at their office, and you are asked a bunch of questions. At the end of an hour or so, you were told that time is up and that you should come back next week for a subsequent appointment. What would that be like for you? (While I am writing this at a cafe, by sheer luck I overheard a man in his late 30s say to his father-in-law, "The psychologist just asked a bunch of questions and charged me 90 bucks. That's simply dishonest.")

While it's important to ask questions to organise yourself and develop clinical formulations of your client, do not prioritise *your* intake. Worry more about our client's intake.

Clients expect at least something they can leave with, be it an idea, a different perspective, or even tangible doses of hope. For better or worse, we must recognise that we cannot *not* influence.

Ask ourselves, "What are we *giving* our clients in the first sessions?"

See also I. **Intake Second (Not First)**, II. **Gifting: Give a Gift.**

3. THE 4P'S VERSUS THE 1P

"Our highest priority is to protect our ability to prioritise"
~ Greg Mckeown, *Essentialism* p. 101.

The Intake Model sees several essentials. While the Engagement Model narrows down to one essential.

The traditional pedagogy based on a biopsychosocial perspective schools us to develop the 4 P's: Predisposing, Precipitating, Perpetuating, and Protective factors about our clients.

We must go beyond that. In order to engage our clients, we must train ourselves to spot *the* essential.

When we have two or more priorities, we lose any sort of focus. In the book *Essentialism*, Greg Mckeown points out that 500 years ago, only the singular pronoun "Priority" existed. It was only at the turn of the 18th century that the plural "priorities" entered our English lexicon.[1]

We have to filter down from 4 P's to 1 P.

What is one thing that my client needs help from me right now and is willing to work on in the first session?

We may start broad, but we cannot end the first session without narrowing things down. The Intake Model exists in a framework that assumes clients are motivated to return for subsequent sessions. The Engagement Model believes that trust is earned and not a given.

The Intake Model assumes there are a couple of priorities at play. The Engagement Model priorities figuring out what is the highest priority. It uses blinders like on a racehorse, not to restrict its vision, but to keep focused. An intentional constraint[2] keeps you focused on your *client's priority*.

In the Engagement Model, *the law of sacrifice*[3]—giving up something of lesser value in order to attain something of greater value —is at work. You might not get to comprehend a person's attachment history if he is experiencing anxiety right now. Neither would you be able to attain a complete psycho-social history and the details of every heartbreak he has encountered.

The Engagement Model is not blind. It recognises that most clients do not just have one problem. It simply orders, ranks, and prioritises. It assumes that our ability to resonate and target their highest concern draws them into the ritual of therapy, one session at a time.

See also **4. Avoid TBU ("True But Useless") Information, 5. Make Clients First, 6. Remove the Gatekeeper...**

4. AVOID TBU ("TRUE BUT USELESS") INFORMATION

A psychotherapist is not an archaeologist.

In the first session, don't go digging around for "true but useless" (TBU) information.[1]

The Intake Model schools us this way: Step 1: Figure out the "clinical" background, who's who in the system. Step 2: Develop a rigorous case formulation. Step 3: Slay our clients with our latest evidence-based interventions.

We do not need to conduct a "thorough psycho-social assessment" before we begin therapy.

Our urge is to gather all the necessary facts from the person. One eminent psychiatrist once said to a room of more than a hundred mental health professionals during a grand ward round, "we must seek the truth out of our patients." I gather he was extolling us to become Sherlock Holmes. While his forensic approach appealed to me, imagine if we adopted this idea in our first sessions in therapy.

Have we earned the license to pry?

If we start a first session like a truth seeker, we run the risk of three problems. First, as we try to dig the past and gather all the facts, we may inadvertently re-traumatise our clients. For example, I was referred by Benjamin's general practitioner (GP) to help him with his post-traumatic stress disorder, regarding a significant event of abuse that happened in his teenage years. Even though it was clearly defined as PTSD by his GP, Benjamin wasn't prepared, nor interested in talking about it in the first session. If I had pushed, insisting that this was *the* primary concern, I would have caused emotional injury. He might have dropped out from therapy.

Second, even as we attempt to gather all the facts in the first session, even if your client responds to your questions, we may not have consensus to delve in a particular area of their life. Returning to Benjamin, I could have stated that I needed some background information about the past traumatic event, even though we wouldn't go to work on it immediately (Do you hear TBU?). By doing this, I run the risk of disembodying his experience in the assessment process. Another time I heard a person come out of a session from a mental health centre and saying to her mom in the waiting room, "Why should I come here and reveal my feelings?! What good does that do, opening up old wounds?" She burst into tears. I would speculate that the therapist and client have not yet formed a consensus about what to talk about.

Finally, the Intake Model not only assumes that there are a handful of priorities but it also fails to commit to an **effective focus**. That is, while we gather TBU, we lose a sense of an emotionally charged purpose of therapy. An Engagement Model develops an effective focus. The sun alone does nothing to a leaf, but when we focus its rays through a magnifying glass, the leaf starts to smoke.

Near the end of the first session, I asked Benjamin, "What are some questions that I have yet to ask you that you deem as important?" Ben said, "I don't know how to phrase it in a question, but I know that I can't change what happened in the past... I just can't seem to make relationships work." Ben was saying that maintaining relationships is a problem for him, and this source of pain is an entry point for him in therapy. Work with that. Don't go digging first. If it's relevant, trust that the issue will unearth itself in the process. It was only in the eighth session that he began to bring up issues relating to the past traumatic events, which was related to his mis-trust in relationships. If I had tried to be efficient and pry further in the first session, he wouldn't have felt emotionally safe to continue therapy.

Developing an emotional bond is still no guarantee of an effective focus. We need to gain consensus on the **process goal** (i.e., the agreement on *how* to go about working through the challenges) and the **outcome goal** (i.e., what the person ultimately wants from treatment). I recall another client some years back, that we both felt that we had a good connection with each other, but ultimately, it didn't translate to good outcomes. Upon review, it struck me that I failed to develop an effective focus throughout the first 15-16 sessions!

Resist the temptation of TBU.

See also **3. The 4P's versus. the 1P.**

5. MAKE THE CLIENT FIRST

Be hospitable. Learn to receive your client like a guest.

I f we de-prioritised an Intake Model in the first session, we can then focus on being a good host. From an Engagement Model, a good host is not only respectful, he is also warm and personable, not cold and rigid.

The word "hospitable" is a derivative of the 16th-century French word *hospiter*, which means to "receive a guest"; to welcome the person. Being hospitable is not being clinical. When we are hospitable, we welcome all parts—the good, the bad, and the ugly. Help them feel comfortable in their chair. Make them a cup of tea if you can. Warm up the human connection. Resist the urge to do a cold-cut psychological intake.

Entrepreneur and writer Derek Sivers once said that people are interesting when you are interested. We may be interested in their past, but we need to be interested in them first. When our friends come over to our home, we don't just dive into their past or their pain. We simply welcome them and engage in small talk.

You might say, "But we don't have the time for that at the clinic." Well, can you afford not to? Like a good host, because this is the first meeting, we address and soothe any anxiety that is present. We attend to how he or she is feeling in the room with you. When I ask a client, "What's it like for you coming to this meeting?" I sometimes get a response about how anxious the patient was as they made the journey to my office. Then I might ask, "What's it like being here right now?" They usually notice feeling tensed. That often leads to a sigh; a discharge of their anxieties. Simply because you called out the elephant in the room, and did not bulldoze them with your intake questions. Others might have a hard time responding to such an intimate question, and might move on to the presenting concerns at hand. In such instances, slow down. Help your client to be present. It can be hard for them, given the circumstance that led them to therapy.

A good host cares about making the person feel comfortable. Even though the conversation is about something painful, you want to take care, much like an empathic nurse who is about to take out the bandage on your five-year-old son's injured knee. She would not hastily rip it out, but would do her best to soothe and distract him, while getting the job done humanely.

A good host is not trying to sell you something. In fact, just think of your many experiences with a sale personnel. We feel repelled by those who are working hard on their pitch, trying to multiply our yes-set responses to them, and hoping to seal the deal. On the contrary, the good salesperson does not behave like a salesperson. They are not trying to be persuasive; they are personable.[1]

If anything, at the end of the first session, help your client feel welcomed. Help them feel welcomed by *you*, as they reveal parts of themselves—warts and all. In turn, this helps them feel better about themselves.

See also **3. The 4P's versus. the 1P.**

6. REMOVE THE GATEKEEPER...

Traditional triaging from an Intake Model sounds like a good idea: Have an intake therapist who "screens" the case anywhere from 30 minutes to an hour, bump them up to a "treating" therapist, based upon their presenting concerns, needs, severity, and urgency.

But there's a problem. People in distress are two to three times more likely to discontinue treatment if they see someone for an initial assessment and are transferred to see another therapist.[1] This is one of those solutions that causes new problems. From an organisational standpoint, it makes perfect sense. Since we have limited resources, we prioritise and slot the clients in accordingly. It's the right thing to do. Screen them. Gatekeep the process before it funnels through to the "treating" therapist.

From a client's standpoint, this is a source of pain. It is a lack of empathic action. Our own perspective blinds us. "Why should I see someone and tell them all my problems, and then get transferred to see someone else, and regurgitate all my problems again?" In the two countries that I've worked in, clients often had to pass through a general practitioner or a psychiatrist before getting to us. The triage officer is yet another hurdle to jump through.

When you are ultimately not the treating therapist, asking clients all those screening assessment questions runs the risk of re-trau-matising the clients.

This is an important issue to confront, given that it causes people to drop out of treatment. This also has huge cost implications for an organisation. A team of 18 researchers led by Steven Lars Nielsen concluded that not only did having an intake assessment not improve outcomes, it also cost the agencies 19% more than clients seen by the same person.[2]

Anything that causes people to lose faith in the process is an alarm we need to take heed. From an Engagement Model, here's what I recommend:

Get the therapist as close as possible to the starting line.

Even if it means seeing the client briefly. If you are a clinical manager in an agency, create one weekly open slot. If you have seven therapists, create one slot per day. That way, clients who are in urgent need to see someone can make a brief structured contact with the therapist themselves. Unless the client has an explicit preference, trying to assign the "right" therapist to fit the client gets you no closer than a chimpanzee drawing a lucky number.[3]

Here's my plea: Remove the gatekeeper.

See also **4. Avoid TBU ("True But Useless") Information, 7. ...If You Can't, Be the Gate Opener.**

7. ...IF YOU CAN'T, BE THE GATE OPENER.

There are agency's priorities and there are clients' priorities. **Triaging must be about prioritising clients' priorities.**

If for some reason, your workplace setting requires a triaging system, like in a large community mental health setting, prioritise **client preferences.** The Intake Model says the primary job of an intake is to "screen" the level of severity and types of problems, and to match client preferences when we can. On the other hand, the Engagement Model says, at the intake session, figure out what your client's worldview and values and have a way to match that in the treatment provided. *Do you have a preference to see a male/female/LGBT therapist? Religious background? Which days can you attend therapy?* An administrative staff can provide help here. If the client has an explicit preference, it's vital we try to match them. Otherwise, point them in the right direction.

The benefits of matching client preferences are huge. It not only prevents premature termination, it reduces costs for clients and treatment centres (i.e., no-shows and re-assigning to another treatment provider), as well as having clients become active collaborators in the treatment process.

We need to attempt to match client preferences before attempting to influence their expectations of therapy. Generally, client preferences fall into three categories: role, therapist, or treatment-type preferences.[1] First, role preferences represent what they expect of their therapists (e.g., advice-giving, active listening, use of homework, individual or group format) and themselves during the course of treatment. Second, therapist preferences include characteristics and beliefs clients hope their treating therapist has (e.g., demographics, age, gender, spiritual orientation). Finally, treatment-type preferences relate to the type of intervention they hope for (e.g., specified or unspecified forms of psychotherapy vs. medication).

Two meta-analyses by Joshua Swift and his colleagues point out that preference accommodation applies to all types of clients, regardless of their diagnosis, ethnicity, age, gender, marital status, and education level.[2] This seems fairly obvious. But we have to reconsider what the researchers are saying due to our cognitive biases. For instance, how easy it is for us to spend our time diagnosing a person and trying to match a particular treatment modality to the diagnosis instead of tuning in to their preferences about therapy.

Here is a table of questions you can use to organise your triaging process according to client preferences:

LIST OF CLIENT PREFERENCES

*Instructions: There are two steps to this process. First, **rate** each of the descriptors provided from 1 to 5. Second, rank the **top 3** in the order of importance. A practitioner can use this as a checklist or clients can also complete this on their own.*

1. **Rating Scale:** *5-point Likert scale (1 = This wouldn't bother me at all and 5 = I would never want to see a therapist if I had to do this)*

2. **Ranking:** *Please rank the Top 3 in this list beginning with the number one thing that you would want in your treatment. Write the number "1" on the line next to the thing that you would want the most from a treatment, a "2" for the second thing you would want the most, and "3" for the third thing you would want the most.[3]*

Descriptors	Notes	Rating (1-5)	Ranking
Frequency (weekly, fortnightly)	Fortnightly only; alternate Mondays. Willing attend on her off-days.	5	2
Time	Anytime.	1	
Location	Same place as triage.	3	
How In-Depth (Talking about very personal details of my life, including talking about my relationships with other people)	Open to sharing details about her life.	2	
Duration of Therapy (Short Term, 10-16 sessions vs. Long Term >20 sessions)	Likely short-term.	3	
Willingness for Homework Assignment	Willing to do tasks provided between-sessions.	2	
Therapist Gender	Nil preference.	1	
Therapist Ethnicity	Nil preference.	1	
Therapist Age	Nil preference.	1	
Therapist Beliefs	Prefers if therapist is open to her spiritual beliefs in Buddhism.	4	3
Medication	Prefers to engage in therapy, but open to medication if needed at a later stage. Needs more information on anti-depressants. Two years ago, she had side-effects from it.	5	1

From the example in this table, given her previous experience, it is evident that this particular client wishes to be engaged in therapy rather than the use of psychopharmaceuticals (see Ranked #1 in the list). She also indicated that she could only attend sessions on her off days (once a fortnight).

Some clients may not know what they want. When you survey the literature, these factors may not even seem to impact treatment outcome. However, for other clients, these factors can be critical. For example, if a client perceives himself to invest only in short-term therapy to resolve a mild anxiety related problem, it would be a mismatch to assign him to a therapist who works only in a long-term psychoanalytic fashion. Similarly, if a female client has recently experienced domestic violence by a partner, she may feel more comfortable to work with a female instead of a male therapist.

Make sure you do not lose your ability to prioritise the factor that makes a difference in outcomes: Client preferences. Learn to ask better questions to understand and match their needs.

See also **6. Remove the Gatekeeper..., 29. Raising Expectations.**

8. JUDGE YOUR ASSESSMENT

Assess Your First Session, Not Your Client.

I t's hard to hear yourself.

It first dawned on me about the importance of hearing yourself when I was playing in a band, and we were recording vocals for a song. It never fails to amaze me, how we hear ourselves differently in the moment, compared with hearing ourselves in a recording. The singer often doesn't realise how he or she sang in a specific part. It's even harder to hear yourself when performing onstage. That's why most artists wear in-ear monitors, so that they can hear themselves and stay in key.

The same goes for therapy. It's hard to listen to what we are doing in the moment. In the session, we are focused on giving our best. In order to get better, we need to counteract flow states, and seek to judge the way we perform, especially in our first sessions.

We need to undo what we have been taught from an Intake Model, that is, to judge our clients. Instead, we need to learn to judge the way we assess first. We see others not as they are, but as we are.

Here's a suggestion: Record your first sessions. Don't trust your case notes or memory when doing this; use an audio or video recording device.[1] Hear what your client is saying explicitly and implicitly. Then, pay attention to how you respond to your client's needs.

Better yet, review those first sessions that clients drop out thereafter. For instance, when you are reviewing a first session that did not convert to a subsequent session, you want to pick out particular points the client disengaged. Reflect on what you could have done to help them put another foot in the door. Was an induction into therapy conducted? Was there a mis-match of expectations? Did you check with the client?

Schedule a time to review the recording. Have your clinical supervisor review this with you. If you can't get a supervisor, grab a colleague you admire to reflect on the first session with you. Resist the urge to watch the recording straight through. Pause the recording every 10 minutes. During that pause, ask yourself, knowing what you know now, how would you respond to the client instead? Ask your supervisor or colleague, "How would you respond?" Then hear how you responded in the recording. Compare and contrast.

There are three main reasons why clients don't return for a second visit. One, they weren't keen to be there to begin with. Usually this is a mandated client, or the person comes at the behest of a family member. Second, through the interaction in the initial session, the client didn't experience the confidence that the session was going to help them. Third, there was no clear and hopeful plan about what to expect in the therapeutic process.

In the first "mandated" scenario, when reviewing the recording, you want to check with yourself, "Did I address the context of 'someone' else (e.g., a judge, parent, spouse) asking him/her to attend this session?"

In the second "low confidence" scenario, when reviewing the recording, ask yourself, "At which point did I lose my client?"

In the third "what to expect" scenario, when reviewing near the end of the recording, ask yourself, "Did I provide a clear rationale of what's up ahead? Did I explicitly convey a sense of deep respect and hope for change?"

It's painful to hear yourself when you are reviewing your recordings. But by doing so, you not only get a chance to review, what you can extract from this will be deeply individualised. Paradoxically, this specific learning will also be generalisable to others clients you work with, especially if you get to the core principles at work. This is important, because, **LEARNING = TRANSFER.** That is, when we acquire new information, and if we make that readily retrievable in our memory, we can then generalise these principles into other related situations.

See also **29. Raising Expectations, 48. A Coach, 51. Performance Feedback Versus Learning Feedback, 55. Recording Your First Sessions.**

9. DO THE PREP

Chance favors the prepared mind. ~ *Louis Pasteur*

I've been given conflicting advice. Some say, read the casenotes before the first session. Others say, go in empty. In practice, I used to oscillate between the two. It became clear to me after listening to a Tim Ferriss interview with renowned strategist, Tony Robbins. He puts it plainly, "Do the prep. Don't be lazy, or make excuses about it..." He goes on to speak about the amount of hours he puts into researching a client before he meets him, so that he can ask better questions about his client in order be helpful.

Since then, I've made sure I did the prep. I figured if my client has taken the step to break their silence with me, I owe it to him or her to go in as prepared as I can. It's like a music performance. Even though it might be an improvisational jazz piece on stage, practice is still needed.

The Intake Model seeks ways to make a clinical diagnosis and profile the persons. When I read the case history, I used to worry about going into the first session with a confirmation bias.

Whereas the Engagement Model suggests a quick way to circumvent this: *Seek the counterfactuals.* "One of the best ways to figure out whether or not you're right is to actively look for information that proves you're wrong," says author Josh Kaufman. If a client was diagnosed with borderline personality disorder (BPD), rather than seek to confirm the diagnosis in the first session, seek evidence for the contrary. "How it is that you maintained such a tight and long-term friendship with Brenda?"

When you read the case history, paint a picture of your client. Jeff Zeig taught me an excellent idea he learned from the renowned psychiatrist and hypnotist Milton Erickson: After you've done your prep, write down your impressions of the person before you see her. Predict how the person would talk, her gait, her level of engagement, her dress, her level of anxiety, etc. Get specific. It's important to write it down, otherwise, we might slip into "I-Knew-It-All-Along" cognitive bias. Once again, seek to be disconfirmed. We listen differently when we are surprised by the contrary.

Doing the prep also means that you psych yourself for the first session. Do you have a ritual before you start? There's much to learn from religious ceremonial practices. You make the sign of the cross, you take off your shoes, you bow, you take a moment of silence before you begin. You don't have to be religious to have a ritual before you begin. Athletes have their rituals.[1] Why shouldn't we? In your practice, maybe it's as simple as clearing your desk, or recomposing yourself in a minute of silence before you begin. These symbolic gestures signify to us that we're *making room* for something that's about to happen. By doing the prep, we make sacred what is secular. We redefine the upcoming encounter with a level of reverence so that we can welcome the person into our space for growth and healing.

See also 54. Now, Let's Play with Feedback.

10. LISTEN IN ORDER TO QUESTION, OR QUESTION IN ORDER TO LISTEN?

You know, if you know the answer, but you don't know the question you are in a bad way. But if you have questions, you will find answers.

~ Salvador Minuchin, 2000.

The Intake Model prescribes that the first session is a "questioning session," or what we call an assessment session. One of the key things you can do to improve your skills in the first session is to listen to the way you ask questions.

When used appropriately, questions are more than an assessment tool. Questions have an emotional impact.

The Intake Model listens in order to question. The Engagement Model questions in order to listen.

The Intake Model see questions solely as a means to assess. The Engagement Model sees questions as means to connect.

A question works like a knife. It can inform you with answers ("Can you tell me about your relationship with Elijah."), and it can act like a reflective tool ("As you think about your relationship, what strikes you right now?"). When used carelessly, questions can have an iatrogenic effect. I once observed a trainee who asked a barrage of risk assessment questions, and saw the client devolve from sitting upright and engaged, to become depressed, disengaged and slumped in his chair.

"Truly smart listening requires truly smart questioning," says business leaders Harry Beckwith and Christine Clifford.[1]

Family therapist and psychiatrist Karl Tomm makes a distinction of four types of questions we can use:[2]

I. LINEAL QUESTIONS:

In the first session, we often think of questions as a way of assessing our clients. "How long have you felt depressed?" "When does your panic attack occurs?"

These "Who, What, When, Where, Why, How" type of questions are primarily to orient the therapist. While necessary, if that's all you do in the first session, your client will leave feeling none the richer.

Here's a common statement I hear from clients who don't return after the first (or even first few) session: "My therapist just asked me a bunch of questions... and that's it."

II. CIRCULAR QUESTIONS:

While the concept of circularity, or the connection of things, lies at the heart of systemic therapy, it is worth understanding, even if you are working with individuals instead of families. In essence, circular questions assume bi-directional causal influence, and are used for exploratory purposes. The effects can be liberating. They assume the inter-connection of everything that is happening. Tomm provides some useful examples.[2] Here's a flavor of circular questions: "Who in the family thinks this is a problem?" "Who worries about you the most?" "What happens between Mom and Dad when Jacob goes against Mom?"

Once I asked a 16-year-old male what happened to him when his parents clashed with each other in a heated argument. He tried to make light of it at first, saying that he wasn't involved in the fight, and it wasn't a big deal. I clarified, "What was it like for *you*—not what happened—when your parents quarreled?" He sighed, and began to share about how he used to hide in his cupboard when his parents were raising their voices and throwing things at each other. From those early experiences he learned to avoid conflicts, which in turn closed him off from the possibility of leading a more fulfilling life.

III. STRATEGIC QUESTIONS:

Unlike lineal and circular questions, strategic questions are aimed to influence. The effect is usually to empower, correct and mobilise a stuck situation. Therapists often talk about staying neutral and non-confrontational. I think this is a mistake. When used judiciously, strategic questions can be therapeutic. Therapists need to own their point of view, *and* be willing to stand corrected; that our perspective can be wrong.

Here are some of Tomm's examples of strategic questions: "Can you see how your withdrawal gets your wife disappointed and frustrated?" "Why don't you talk to him (husband) about your worries instead of the kids?"

In my practice, I found making distinctions to be a helpful theme in strategic questions: "Instead of *worrying*, what happens if you start *planning*? Can you see the difference?" "What happens if we transform your judging mindset into a *learning* mindset?"

IV. REFLEXIVE QUESTIONS:

Reflexive questions combine the best of circular and strategic questions. Their effect is to generate possibilities and open up spaces. "These questions are reflexive in that they are formulated to trigger family members to reflect upon the implications of their current perceptions and actions and to consider new options," says Tomm.[2]

Examples of reflexive questions:

> To a family: "How can everyone keep connected with Tammy (daughter), even if she meets with setbacks again?"
> To father and son: "What do you appreciate most about your father? What do you appreciate most about your son?"
> To a couple: "What does he/she bring out in you that you like about yourself?"
> To an individual: "Who in the family would be most surprised about how you are discovering yourself?"

Questions are more than just a way to elicit information or to assess. When we ask a question, use it as a way to relate. When we relate in a deeply personal way, we potentiate the possibility of healing.

Theologian Nelle Morton says, "Our job is to hear the person into speech." Slow down. Give your client the time to process your questions. Likewise, take the time to let your client's response sink in. Avoid para-phrasing immediately (e.g., "It sounds like..."). Take it in. Then reflect. Resist the temptation to sound smart.

When we take the time to reflect on the answer, it shows that you treat the client with reverence. Have you ever been with someone who asked you questions after questions and it just didn't seem like they were interested in your response, but more in getting the next question out of their head?

Question in order to listen.

See also **8. Judge Your Assessment, 37. Healing Questions.**

11. GIFTING: GIVE A GIFT

I once attended a wedding where the couple gave wine glasses with their names on it. The problem with this sort of gift is that it's focused on the giver, not the receiver. It basically says, "Here's a memory of the wedding couple."

Another wedding couple decided to create a photo booth and have professionals take photos of their guests as memorabilia. This was a hit, because this gift was focused on the *receiver*. Guests are more likely to keep this souvenir. It basically says, "Here's a memory of *you*."

Likewise with your first sessions. Don't just give the client your name card or an appointment card. Give them something that is for *them*. I once heard that the renowned psychiatrist and hypnotherapist Milton Erickson used to give objects from his room to his clients, so that they can have a tangible association of the work in therapy.[1]

While you need not give your prized possessions to all your clients, you can give them one of the following:

I. A Story
II. An Aphorism/Equation
III. A Symbol

Giftings impact your clients' prospective memory.

Memory is often talked about in retrospective terms. What you want to do with your gifting, which often happens as a way to close the session, is to influence your client's *future* recall of the first meeting with you.

I. A STORY

We are creatures of stories. We make sense of our lives in coherent narratives. Stories speak to your clients via the road of metaphors. When we provide a relevant story, fable, or parable, clients may be able to resonate with it and find parallels in their way of resolving their problems.

Talking about *A* can lead to change in *B*. When we employ stories for a therapeutic purpose, the client can draw from such analogies, allowing them to make inferences and meaning with regards to their concerns.[2]

Here's one story I like to tell in the first session, especially if the person is facing an existential crisis:

> *A farmer had only one horse. One day, his horse ran away.*
> *His neighbors said, "I'm so sorry. This is such bad news. You must be so upset."*
> *The man just said, "We'll see."*
> *A few days later, his horse came back with twenty wild horses following. The man and his son corralled all 21 horses.*

*His neighbors said, "Congratulations! This is such good news.
You must be so happy!"
The man just said, "We'll see."
One of the wild horses kicked the man's only son, breaking both
his legs.
His neighbors said, "I'm so sorry. This is such bad news. You
must be so upset."
The man just said, "We'll see."
The country went to war, and every able-bodied young man
was drafted to fight. The war was terrible and killed every
young man, but the farmer's son was spared, since his broken
legs prevented him from being drafted.
His neighbors said, "Congratulations! This is such good news.
You must be so happy!"*

The man just said, "We'll see."[3]

II. AN APHORISM/EQUATION

Before you wrap up the session, write down on an aphorism or a simple equation on an index card for your client. This creates a memorable imprint of the session. Give this to your client. An aphorism is "a statement of truth or opinion expressed in a concise and witty manner."[4] An equation can help capture the essence of a subject based on the relationship between different variables. I'd provide two vignettes to illustrate this.

First example: I once worked with a teacher who was experiencing burnout. Even though he had a deep passion to reach out to the less academic students, who most teachers write off as failures, he was crestfallen by failing to bring up the test scores of his class; he blamed himself. At the end of the first session, I wrote on an index card the following:

"Failing is not the same as Failure."

And then I said, "You know this lesson well. The best teachers are also good students." He kept quiet. He got it. He looked at me. He said, "I know this. But I never really took it to heart." We both agreed that this was the time in his life to teach his heart what his head already knew.

Second example: I was asked to see a 16-year-old female who was depressed and self-harming. She had been seen by previous counsellors and was flagged as being "emotionally dysregulated" (a current catchphrase). I had to figure out what was going on in her life that was hurting her. It turned out that her parents were separating, and that she had just lost her horse. In line with "Follow the Spark" and "Follow the Pain" (see respective chapters), I asked her about her relationships with horses. Seven minutes into the initial session, this was the turning point of the conversation. She began to tell me about her involvement in equestrian riding, the farm that her father ran, and the horses that she attempted to save on a weekly basis from the slaughterhouse. She went at length to tell me on how she trained horses: "You can't use brute force to make them listen to you. You have to work with them. They sense your fear... You gotta attune... Go slow... give them space. And bond with them."

I would never say this to another client. But I decided to whip out a post-it note and wrote the following:

"Horses = Emotions"

Then I said, "Treat your emotion the way you treat horses." She got it. It would have made no sense to another person. But given the emergent theme of our conversation, it seemed befitting. It may have not. If it didn't, I would simply abandon ship. Never be wedded to your gifts. They're meant to be given away.

As we closed our therapy engagement at the eighth session, this theme came back full circle, as we shared about a book she was writing as a tribute to her Nan (grandmother) who taught her to ride at a young age. She revealed how her previous counsellors told her that talking about horses was "irrelevant" to the therapy. She was upset. She said, "What the heck do you mean? Horses are my life!" This time, I wrote down an improved equation, "Horses = You = Nan." Then I said, "Continue to grow your life, as your Nan and horses have given you life."

One caveat. Avoid cliches like "paradigm shift," "think outside the box," or "less is more." If it sounds trite, your client might feel patronised.

III. SYMBOLS

Images that capture the gist of a vital takeaway point speak at an emotional than a cognitive level. I once drew a sketchy diamond on an index card for a youth. As she previously talked about how vulnerable she felt opening up her inner world to her ex-boyfriend, I asked her whether she agreed that her feelings were like a precious stone. She said, "Yes." "Then we need to learn to protect it," I added. "And share with the other person only when you can trust him with something so precious."

I worked with a registered nurse who was referred to me by her GP due to panic attacks. She was plagued with guilt over a minor accidental neglect of a patient. We went through a couple of behavioral strategies to help her cope with the bouts of anxiety. Then I drew on an index card a shape of a heart, and scribbled in the centre of it, "Heart out." I said to her, "It seems to me the anti-dote to healing your anxiety attacks is to reach out. In some spiritual practices, they call it 'atonement' or 'making things right.'" I went on to tell stories about a bunch of soldiers who were so guilt-ridden for the killings they committed, that the only way they could begin the healing, was to take up the call to action to atone. So they went back to Cambodia and stayed with the community for a month and helped out in whatever way they could. Even though they couldn't find the families that were directly affected by the warfare of the past, they felt this was their act of repentance. It wasn't enough to think themselves out of it. They needed to act. At the 19th session, she said that the heart symbol from the first session stood out for her. Although she eventually left the nursing profession, she formed a small business forging her love for art and social service by reaching out to the community.

We illuminate with the use of stories, aphorisms/equations and symbols. This creates a meaningful and sustaining impact on our clients, with something they can hold on to.

See also **24. Follow the Pain, 25. Follow the Spark, 41. How to Close A First Session.**

12. SECULARISE SPIRITUALITY

W hen we speak of spirituality, we are really speaking about our sense of self.

I urge you to talk about your client's beliefs[1]. You might say you don't have one. That's fine. That's your belief. For your client, discerning God's will might be crucial in helping them seek direction, or they might believe that "things happen for a reason."

By speaking of spirituality, we can better appreciate how our clients' beliefs govern how they see others, themselves, and the way that they live.

I come from an Asian culture that is informed by a variety of practices. In Singapore, I see a fervent Christian in one session, and a Buddhist-Taoist who believes in spirit possession the next, followed by a devout Muslim, and then a staunch atheist to close the day.

I once saw a client in his 30s who migrated from China to Singapore to work as a labourer. He talked about his experience of a panic attack on his wedding day. Based on his family's religious practices, he experienced a spirit possession by his late grandfather. He couldn't quite make sense whether this was a purely psychological issue of freaking out on his wedding day, or a possession that he was resisting because he was not keen on carrying on the tradition of being a spirit medium in his family. In the initial session, my task is to hold both worlds with deep respect.

A religious Protestant Christian in his 40s was referred to me because of severe depression. He was highly ruminative, plagued with a sense of "analysis paralysis." When I enquired about his background, he told me about his previous involvement in his church community. His view of the problem was that he no longer felt "moved by the spirit." I asked him about this.

"I think it's because, five years ago, I failed to listen to God's call to give up my life and serve the church as a missionary." Again, I asked, "So you are saying that God is punishing you for not following his call?"

"Yes," he replied.

"We know of a 'jealous God' in the Old Testament. Where is the forgiving God we see in Christ in the New Testament?" I added, "What happens if you forgive yourself too?"

While some professionals might label this client as clinically depressed, we can better appreciate the person if we see it as a spiritual crisis and help his through self-forgiveness. The Intake Model does not embody the topic of spirituality. The Engagement Model embraces our client's belief system.

In Australia, I worked with an agnostic female in her 40s. Though she didn't practice in a formal religion, she believed that "everything happens for a reason." Going with this lens in the initial session, I then helped her to reevaluate significant losses and setbacks in her life. That is, in times of crisis, instead of asking herself, "What's wrong with me?" which has been making her depressed, she can ask herself a better question, "What is Life trying to teach you?" A shift in the question put her on an entirely a different quest.

You might be thinking, why can't I refer the client to spiritual counsel instead? You can, and in some instances, you should. Remember, the key here is that you want to tap into your client's beliefs, and utilise them in the therapeutic engagement. You do not want to create false dichotomies between psychology and spirituality. After all, the *psyche* means the soul.

The most soulful thing to do is to speak of the sacred in our secular conversation. In turn, we make our conversations sacred.

See also **19.** **"What is Your View of the Problem?", 22. Frame It.**

13. ASSESSING RISK FROM BOTH SIDES

Some years ago, I was in a grand ward round meeting in a psychiatric hospital. A full multidisciplinary team of 50-odd mental health professionals was present to witness a discussion of a case. A senior psychiatrist led the presentation. The patient (let's call him Eric) was a man in his early forties who had been severely depressed, and had been brought in by his family against his will to seek treatment. He had already been in the in-patient facility for close to two weeks. Summoned by the nurse, Eric came into the crowded room, obviously anxious. As usual, the senior psychiatrists assigned a junior or trainee psychiatrist to conduct a face-to-face interview with the patient, while the rest of us watch on.

What transpired left a mark on me. Eric tried his best to calm his nerves and remained polite and sat upright. The medical officer began his interview without much fanfare, and opened the flood-gates of risk assessment questions. "Have you thought of killing yourself?" "Do you have any plans?" "Have you attempted in the past?" "Why did you do it?" The patient was crumbling in front of us. The medical officer continued his risk assessment checklist.[1]

Not only did he fail to acknowledge the potential shame Eric might have felt revealing his private thoughts in front of the audience, but the psychiatrist also failed to see that the impact of his questions had directly induced a state of depression, causing Eric to withdraw back into his shell.

While I imagine a therapy session to be different to a psychiatric interview, we fail to see the effects of our questions and the way we ask them. For example, after asking about Eric's suicidal ideation, the psychiatrist could have added, "What has kept you alive, in spite of the difficulties you have been facing?" This could have at the very least counterbalanced the interview. It could have also helped Eric shared another part of himself that he rarely spoke about.

Assess for risks and resources.[2]

Despite our confidence in our assessments, we are no good at predicting suicides.[3] In other words, the questions asked by the psychiatrist in the above example holds little predictive value. If we are not good at forecasting the level of risk, we might as well attempt to balance the scales. When we are intentional, our questions have a powerful impact.

See also 10. Listen in Order to Question, or Question in Order to Listen? 24. Follow The Pain, 25. Follow the Spark, 37. Healing Questions.

14. GET OVER THE SACRED COW OF "ADHERING TO THE MODEL"

"People don't want to buy a quarter-inch drill. They want a quarter-inch hole!"
~ Theodore Levitt, business school marketing professor.

The most difficult time to advise a clinician to not focus on an approach is after his attendance at a therapy workshop. A therapist who has recently returned from a somatic-informed workshop can't help but focus on the body. Another therapist who completed training in emotion-focused approach will bias towards digging into primary and secondary emotions, or exploring unfinished business. Recency and self-referential biases are always at play.

A meta-analysis of 36 studies indicated that adherence and competence to a particular approach in therapy account for "very close to zero" towards client outcomes.[1] More recently, a study found that more flexible therapists attain better outcomes with their clients, compared with therapists who are less flexible in their adherence to their approach in therapy.[2]

These findings sound intuitive. Education researchers John

Hattie and Gregory Yates warn that we must not confuse clarity with triviality.[3] We require clarity in things we hold as a priority. The priority of the first session is the engagement of our clients.

While it might be useful to attend a variety of trainings and workshops to amass ideas, metaphors and methods to stack up our toolbox, let's not get lost. Focus on what motivates your client. Tap into how they see the world. What is their view of the problem? What is their pain point? What are the sparks in their life?

I'm not talking about this through the lens of integrating models, or attempting to be pluralistic. I hear some voices saying, "But you gotta be good at one or two key therapy models in order to deliver evidence-based work." The Intake Model assumes the need to be competent at a particular school of thought. Recall: Competence and adherence to particular approaches do not create better outcomes. Instead, from an Engagement Model, think about getting good at creating quarter-inch holes, instead of getting obsessed with drill bits.

After more than 50 years as a highly acclaimed songwriter with the Beatles, the Wings, and a solo career, Paul McCartney started a songwriting class in a school he helped to revive in Liverpool. Here's what Sir McCartney said to his students, "I don't know how to do this. You would think I do, but it's not one of these things you ever know how to do. "[4] I don't think he's trying to be modest, though he must have vexed his students with his response. He went on to explain the importance of being willing to mess around, follow a chord, a lyric or a beat that allures you in the moment.

There is no formula. If there is, you probably should be abandoning it.

Milton Erickson offers a useful proposition. Create a new approach with every new client. "Each person is a unique individual. Hence, psychotherapy should be formulated to meet the uniqueness of the individual's needs, rather than tailoring the person to fit the Procrustean bed of a hypothetical theory of human behavior."

There is no formula, but there is a *form* in creating a good first session. The Intake Model subscribes to an assessment formula. The Engagement Model says to develop a structure to increase the emotional impact with each client. Develop principles of how to increase engagement and not adherence. Go into the first session with a compass as a guide, and not with a pre-defined map of how you should proceed.

Like the astute jazz improviser, wait to see who your client is and what he or she presents. Use who they are and what they bring. And then bring your gifts to the table. An improviser is prepared, just not wedded to any ideology or rigid plans.

Become highly competent as a therapist, not in a school of therapy.

See also 3. 4P's versus the 1P, 19. "What is Your View of the Problem?", 21. Define the Lead Story, 24. Follow the Pain, 25. Follow the Spark.

SUMMARY OF INTAKE MODEL VS. ENGAGEMENT MODEL

L et's consolidate the key distinctions between an Intake Model versus an Engagement Model of a first session:

Chapters	Intake Model	Engagement Model
1. Intake Second (Not First)	Thorough clinical assessment.	Create a climate of deep engagement.
2. The Perils of an Intake Model	Take.	Give.
3. The 4P's versus The 1P	Priorities.	Priority.
4. Avoid TBU ("True But Useless Information")	Elicit "True But Useless" Information.	Develop an effective focus.
5. Make The Client First	Being clinical.	Being a good host.
6. Remove the Gatekeeper...	Create a gatekeeper for triage.	Remove the gate.
7. ...If You Can't, Be The Gate Opener.	Match client preferences when we can.	Client preferences is *the* priority.
8. Judge Your Assessment	Judge your client.	Judge your assessment.
9. Do The Prep	Seek to confirm what you know.	Be prepared to be wrong.
10. Listen in Order to Question, or Question in Order to Listen?	Listen in order to question.	Question in order to listen.
11. Gifting: Give a Gift	Do not intervene.	Give something to hold on to.
12. Secularise Spirituality	Stay secular.	Get spiritual.
13. Assessing Risk From Both Sides	Assess for risks.	Assess for risks and resources.
14. Get Over The Sacred Cow of "Adhering to The Model"	Adhere to the formula of a model.	Develop a *form* to increase engagement.

SECTION II: INCREASE YOUR IMPACT

Define Your Client's Circle of Development.

Work on improving the process that is *influenceable* and *predictive* of outcomes.

Create an impactful emotional memory of the first session.

INTRODUCTION TO INCREASING YOUR IMPACT

In the previous section Breaking the Sacred Rules, I provided an alternative to the traditional Intake Model in the first sessions of psychotherapy, called the Engagement Model. In this section, we will cover key principles on how to increase the level of impact you make in a first session with your clients.

Focusing solely on outcomes is not going to get you better outcomes. Instead, we need to work on improving what is *influenceable* and *predictive* of outcomes: Engagement. To enhance engagement levels right from the word go, we need to facilitate ways that can create an emotional impact.

As we start to engage with our clients in the first session, have our eyes on the growth edge of our clients, and provide direction for the road ahead.

15. FIGURE OUT YOUR CLIENT'S CIRCLE OF DEVELOPMENT

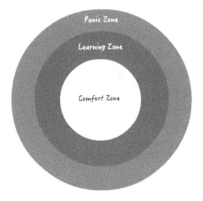

Acouch potato is probably not likely the happiest person on earth. More than likely, when a client ends up at your office, his comfort zone has become a "discomfort" zone.

Our task is to help our clients move from the comfort zone into the learning zone.

This is otherwise known in psychology as the zone of proximal development (ZPD).[1] We are wired to grow. Our learning zone is an optimal threshold where we reach *just beyond* our current ability. This sweet spot is where growth happens.

This is where things get tricky. While it's important to help a client move out of their comfort zone and into their learning zone, we also need to figure out where their *panic zone* is. That is, the tipping point where they get overwhelmed and start to fight, flight, freeze or fall asleep.

We often hear others say, get out of your comfort zone. But where to? If we don't define the learning zone, we might unwittingly tip our clients into a panic zone.

"Follow your heart," "Pursue your passion," these platitudes lack specificity to guide a person on what they need to do to get to where they want to go.

A useful place to start is to ask your client, "What do you want to learn to get better at in your life right now?" This question implies a locus of control in the endeavor, while providing a sense of focus in therapy.

Other similar questions:

"What do you want to improve on in your life?"

"What do you need to be focusing on so as to feel better about yourself?"

For example, a person dealing with social anxiety might naturally define his comfort zone as "staying at home, away from others." What's crucial is to articulate what their learning zone is, and figure out what their panic zone is now. We might think it's important to step out of their isolated comfort zone and connect with others in a behavioral exposure type of approach. But the activity that is curative, is also the thing that he avoids. So the terrain of a learning zone requires further distinctions, such as, "I want to stay focused on feeding my curiosity and not ruminate on what others think of me when I ask a question in class."

Likewise, having clarity about what is panic zone material now is crucial. "To go up to a girl and chat with her," might be overwhelming at first. Labeling activities as panic zone material are not meant to limit. But to intentionally constrain. Constraints help to contain our efforts, and stay focused on what's possible, and not get lost and overwhelmed. A good learning system must not only tell you where to go, but also tell you where *not* to go for the time being.

Help your clients work out their circle of development.

See also 19. "What is Your View of the Problem?", 20. The Goal May be to Figure Out a Goal, 21. Define the Lead Story.

16. HOW DO YOU START A FIRST SESSION? ORIENT.

There are three key things you want to do to organise you and your client in the first session: Orient, reveal yourself, and regulate in-the-moment anxiety. I devote one chapter to each of them.

Orient your client in space and time. Tell them about your office and your administrative process. Explicitly state to your client that this room is to be *their* space during the therapy hour.

"In the next hour, I want you to treat this space as yours. I want you to feel emotionally comfortable and safe being here with me. And you don't have to answer all of my questions if you don't feel ready to talk about them."

Don't let your client begin to pour their troubles immediately without some form of orienting. You want to help them feel contained.

I'd also use this time to tell them about my two quirks in my practice. The first is the use of routine outcome measures to make sure we are on track, and second is the use of audio/video recordings. (More on this in Section III.)

I sometimes use this opportunity to orient myself. I ask them how they found out about our services, who referred them to my practice, and whether they had previous experience in therapy, and I ask my clients to tell me about themselves (aside from the problem that led them to therapy).

After the usual confidentiality and other administrative issues, you may want to consider the following statement to orient your client for the first session: *"I'll be asking you some questions today so that I can figure out if I can be of help to you. At times, the questions are for both you and me to think about... you don't have to feel like you need to know the right answer. At the end of today, I may be giving some of my feedback to you, assigning some tasks to get you engaged in between sessions, etc. Finally, please feel free to ask me anything as we go along. How does that sound to you?"*

Back in Singapore, I once had a client who rushed into the initial session because she missed her bus. It was just past lunchtime, so I asked her if she had eaten.[1] She told me that she didn't have the time to eat. I told her that she should go to the canteen and get a bite before we started. And so she did, though initially hesitant. She was worried about keeping me waiting. I told her that I'd rather have her spend that 10 minutes taking care of herself than for us to ignore her growling stomach while we attempted to feed her mind, which wasn't going to work. She laughed. (Incidentally, the theme of self-neglect transpired to be a predominant piece in our work ahead).

Orienting is not only about feeding your client information. It's about setting the stage for the work ahead.

See also **17. How Do You Start a First Session? Reveal Yourself, 18. How Do You Start a First Session? Regulate In-the-Moment Anxiety, 44. The Use of Routine Outcomes Monitoring, 55. Recording Your First Sessions.**

17. HOW DO YOU START A FIRST SESSION? REVEAL YOURSELF

The purpose of revealing yourself is to establish an immediate, deep and personal connection with the person in front of you. The Brafman brothers termed this magical moment as "click."[1] Social psychology experiments demonstrate that when you open up about yourself *first*, the other party is more likely to warm up to you, and they are more likely to reveal themselves to you.[2]

Be vulnerable first. Tell your clients about you. Not just the dry facts. Humanise the information that you share.

Though some might say this is a matter of preference, I would encourage you to share bits of yourself to your client at the start of therapy. A study by a team of psychologists from the University of Texas at Arlington found that asking questions and self-disclosures among both parties builds a sense of trust.[3] It's not rocket science to figure this out. However, some might hold the belief that you shouldn't taint the picture with your story in therapy. I disagree. Therapy is an endeavor of two or more persons. "It takes two to know one," says Gregory Bateson. If you want your client to open up, show them how you do it. This can have a disarming effect.

Volunteer as much information about yourself as you're comfortable with (how long you've been in practice, married/single, interests, etc.). In fact, say in a sentence or two what brought you to your profession. This is an introduction, so introduce yourself.

Since I'm an ethnic minority working in a western country at my current setting, I tell my clients briefly about my background. I make fun of my stubborn Singaporean accent, and let them know that they should ask me to repeat myself if I'm not clear.

Remember, this isn't about you. Saying something about yourself is about creating mutual trust. This goes a long way, especially with clients who treat you as an "expert," call you "Doctor," or has difficulties trusting others.

Quaker teacher and writer Parker Palmer once said, "Everyday, in every one of our relationships, human beings are asking a simple question. And that question is: 'Is the person that I'm relating to here, more or less the same on the inside, as he or she appears to be on the outside?'"[4] Help your clients through this wandering.

See also **16. How Do You Start a First Session? Orient, 18. How Do You Start a First Session? Regulate In-the-Moment Anxiety.**

18. HOW DO YOU START A FIRST SESSION? REGULATE IN-THE-MOMENT ANXIETY

In the first session, I often ask, "What is it like for you to be here right now?" The reason for this question is for my client to be fully aware of and be in contact with their in-the-moment experience. For some, anxiety is present.

Help your clients to be fully present, moment-by-moment.

Simply asking this question helps them acknowledge the pent-up tension, and there might be an emotional discharge of the anxiety, often with a sigh.[1] On several occasions, I've had clients in the first session start to tear up at this point, almost as if asking that question permitted them to feel what they feel.

Others try to ignore their present inner experience, and press on with trying to get the session "moving forward." They remain tensed. If so, you want to slow them down. Help them regulate their anxiety.

"I noticed that there's a sense of wanting to 'get on with it.' Am I mistaken here?"

"No, you are right. I just want to get down to resolving my issues," says the client.

"Yes. I can understand that. Do you notice that when I asked you how you were feeling right now, it's almost like you ignored checking in with yourself. You ignored you."

"Hmmm... No. I didn't see that."

"It's like... you are dominated by an urgency..." (The client starts to tear... facial muscles begin to slacken from tension, and she lets out a sigh).

Client says, "Yeah... I do. There's always this sense of pressure to do this, and do that... Like I can't get any relief just to breathe."

At times, you might get clients who look utterly frozen when you ask them about their present feelings, as if they were holding their breath. If this happens, I'd immediately help them to regulate their anxiety. "Do you notice that you sort of froze up when I asked you how you are feeling being here with me right now?"

"Yes."

"It's wonderful that you can notice that this is happening inside you. Do you notice what the experience of anxiety is like in your body right now?"

"In my shoulders, it's really tensed. And my stomach is like a knot..."

"Excellent. That's anxiety. Do you notice you are holding your breath, as if you are getting ready to take a deep dive into the ocean?"

"Yes!" Client replies.

"Now, take a few moments to simply breathe easy. Take some

slow natural breaths in... and out." (I'd pace my words to match her rhythm of inhalation and exhalation).

Being able to orient, to reveal some parts of yourself and to regulate anxiety, is necessary groundwork. If you skip these steps, you might find yourself needing to backpedal, or worse still, you might begin to face —what we love to call —"resistance."

See also **16. How Do You Start a First Session? Orient, 17. How Do You Start a First Session? Reveal Yourself.**

19. "WHAT IS YOUR VIEW OF THE PROBLEM?"

"Curiosity never killed the cat."
~ *Journalist and writer, Studs Terkel*

Perspective taking is never as powerful as perspective getting. Too often we ask questions that fuel our perspective taking, and then we formulate some abstract conceptualisation of the person and the problem. Our perspective taking is often limited. Here's what Nicholas Epley, author of Mindwise has to say:

> "The weakness of perspective taking is obvious: it relies on your ability to imagine, or take, the other person's perspective accurately. If you don't really know what it's like to be poor, in pain, suicidally depressed, at the bottom of your corporate ladder, on the receiving end of waterboarding, in the throes of solitary confinement, or to have your source of income soaked in oil, then the mental gymnastics of putting yourself in someone else's shoes isn't going to make you any more accurate. In fact, it might even decrease your accuracy."[1]

Ask your clients, "What is your view of the problem?" "From your perspective, how do you think the problem developed? What do you think caused it?" "What is that like for you?"

For this to work, put down your therapist hat. Think like a journalist. Our clinical training might be to blame. We tend to equate training our empathy skills with learning to "put yourself in the person's shoes." Instead, as Roman Krzanaric wrote in his book *Empathy,* the most potent form of empathic introspection is outrospection. And to have outrospection, we need to learn *perspective getting.*[2] Never fail to ask clients perspective getting questions at the first session.

See also 1. Intake Second (Not First), 8. Judge Your Assessment, 10. Listen in Order to Question, or Question in Order to Listen?

20. THE GOAL MAY BE TO FIGURE OUT THE GOAL

Some therapists assume that a client needs to have a goal before therapy can proceed. If the client has no goal, we write them off as unmotivated.

Sometimes, the goal *is* to figure out a goal.

And don't expect goals to stay the same. They evolve. For the first session, begin by planting seeds of exploration about what your client is aiming for in therapy. I once heard a designer say this: good designers always define and re-define the problem. We ought to borrow that idea.

Too often, people connote goals as something to achieve and do in the future. Entrepreneur Derek Sivers offers a useful counter-point:[1]

> **Good goals are not about the future. Good goals are about changing your *current* actions.**

In other words, let your client's goals organise and change both your behaviors right now.

Sometimes you may need to re-define the goals simply because your client may have a different need than the referring person has in mind. This referring person could be a GP, psychiatrist, the court, or a parent. I once made a mistake of thinking that we ought to work on a presenting concern highlighted by the referring psychiatrist. Because I held a deep respect for this particular psychiatrist, I didn't question it. He thought his patient needed help in his compulsive checking behavior. Right there, I made an attribution error. I wasted the first session attempting to work with the client based on an assumption. I later learned that he was more motivated about rebuilding his relationship with his son.

The following three chapters are aimed to help you form specific goals.

See also **21. Define the Lead Story, 22. Frame It, 23. Gaining Consensus.**

21. DEFINE THE LEAD STORY

"The most important thing is to figure out what is the most important thing."~ Shunryu Suzuki, 1970.

This story, "The Best Journalism Teacher I Ever Had,"[1] by Nora Ephron has been reprinted in other contexts. It is worth sharing here in its entirety.

The best teacher I ever had was named Charles Simms, and he taught journalism at Beverly Hills High School in 1956 and 1957. He was young, cute in an owlist way — crew cut, glasses, etc. — and was a gymnast in the 1956 Olympics. He was also the first person any of us knew who had stereo earphones, and he taught us all to play mahjong.

The first day of journalism class, Mr. Simms did what just about every journalism teacher does in the beginning — he began to teach us how to write a lead. The way this is normally done is that the teacher dictates a set of facts and the class attempts to write the first paragraph of a news story about them. Who, what, where, when, how and why. So he read us a set of facts. It went something like this:

'Kenneth L. Peters, principal of Beverly Hills High School,
announced today that the faculty of the high school will travel
to Sacramento on Thursday for a colloquium on new teaching
methods. Speaking there will be anthropologist Margaret
Mead, educator Robert Maynard Hutchins, and several others.'
We all began typing, and after a few minutes we turned in our
leads. All of them said approximately what Mr. Simms had
dictated, but in the opposite order ("Margaret Mead and Robert
Maynard Hutchins will address the faculty," etc.). Mr. Simms
riffled through what we had turned in, smiled, looked up and
said:
"The lead to the story is, 'There will be no school Thursday.'"
It was an electrifying moment. So that's it, I realized. It's about
the point. The classic newspaper lead of who-what-where-
when-how-and-why is utterly meaningless if you haven't
figured out what the significance of the facts is. What is the
point? What does it mean? He planted those questions in my
head.
And for the year he taught me journalism, every day was like
the first; every assignment, every story, every set of facts he
provided us had a point buried in it somewhere if you looked
hard enough. He turned the class into a gorgeous intellectual
game, and he gave me an enthusiasm for the profession that I
have never lost. Also, of course, he taught me something that
works just as well in life as it does in journalism.
After teaching at Beverly Hills High School for two years,
Charles Simms quit and opened a chain of record stores in Los
Angeles. I hope he's a millionaire.

I suspect that when I've failed to carry the therapeutic work from
the first session into the next was because I failed to define the
lead.

While psychotherapy is not journalism, we certainly can benefit from the concept of defining the lead. When a client comes to our office, we need to sift through the facts and develop an understanding of what's vital for this person. For example, if a client comes to see you due to panic attacks, don't immediately assume that panic attacks are the lead. The panic symptoms may instead hint at what's important.

I'm not saying to ignore the primary symptoms and work on something "deeper." A person with panic symptoms may need some skills to cope with the immediate problem. What I'm emphasising here is that we need to figure out the chorus—the lead story—one person at a time.

For instance, regarding panic attacks, one person's lead story could be developing a deeper relationship with his aging father, while another could be redefining her career path, so that she is doing something meaningful in her life.

Other times, your client may not know their lead story. Then the most important thing for you and your client is to figure that out. (See the previous chapter).

A client's lead story is their true north. Figure this out, and you are on your way to a remarkable journey with your client.

See also **3. The 4Ps vs. The 1P, 20. The Goal May be to Figure Out the Goal, 24. Follow the Pain, 25. Follow the Spark.**

22. FRAME IT

"The most important thing in art is the frame... you have to put a
"box" around it because otherwise, what is that shit on the wall?"
~ Frank Zappa, in Creators on Creating, 1997 p. 196.

You want the person to come out of the first session with a different frame of her problem. You want your client not only to put the issue into context, but also to see the problem in nuanced and cogent terms.

Michael Yapko, a brilliant clinician and teacher in hypnosis, talked about his experience as a supervisee with the founding father of strategic psychotherapy, Jay Haley. While Yapko was trying to describe a "complex" client's psychopathology in rich clinical terms, so that his supervisor could offer some advice, Haley replied, "I wouldn't let her have those problems!"[1]

In other words, frame a problem in solvable terms.

"Solvable" must mean that the definition of the problem should make sense to your client by the end of the first session, even if she doesn't see it at first. Be prepared to "re-frame" it, especially when your client doesn't fully resonate with it.

Remember, **you are the frame-maker. They are the artist.** Your frame must make their art shine.

Move from an Old "Default" Frame to a New Frame.

Old Frame	New Frame
Depressed	Grieving the loss of a significant relationship.
Depressed	Being self-critical.
Depressed	Seeking perfection; no room for failing.
Panic Attack	Overworked, stressed, and a lack of sleep.
Panic Attack	Intimacy triggered off suppressed memory of sexual abuse as a child.
Social Anxiety	Fear of being seen as a loser.
Generalised Anxiety	Fear of feelings.
Generalised Anxiety	Fear of being abandoned.
OCD	Feelings of guilt about past wrongdoings.
OCD	Worries about something bad happening to loved ones.
Borderline Personality Disorder	Difficulty building trust with people that they care about.

Frame the problem in such a way that complements the person. For example, if your client presents as socially anxious, provide an explanation of your perspective (e.g., "You worry of the possibility of others seeing you as awkward... Do you agree?" If so, expand on the price of the worry. "What has this cost you? How long have you suffered because of this?") Then, take the time to honor the symptoms. Take a pro-symptom perspective[2], so that the client can learn to see the symptom's previous function in her life. Ask your client to complete the following sentence: "If I cared less about what others think of me..." Your client might say,

"I might let things slip. Then people might see that I'm less than I am." Helping your client give a voice of emotional truth to the function of her symptoms can have a powerful releasing effect[3].

Hold on a second. Isn't this chapter about case conceptualisation or what others might call clinical formulation? Maybe. Except it isn't as "comprehensive." Its main job isn't to provide a thorough bio-psychosocial explanation, accounting for all the "predisposing, precipitating, perpetuating, and protective factors." Rather, its purpose is to intentionally strip away all that isn't essential.

Remember, the "frame" can evolve and change. A person who presented with depressed mood may be defined as being self-critical at first. After working through this challenge, a more nuanced theme of "I cannot fail" might emerge from the conversation. At that point, the frame can provide new targets to work on perfectionism.

See also **3. The 4 Ps versus the 1 P, 19. "What's Your View of the Problem," 20. The Goal May be to Figure Out the Goal, 21. Define the Lead Story.**

23. GAINING CONSENSUS

After you have framed the problem in solvable terms, make sure you ask your client, "Does this way of seeing the problem make sense to you?" If your client says yes, then ask "Are you **willing** to work on this?"

Without their will on board, you might face several roadblocks. If you are the only willing party involved, you might start to feel that you are doing most of the heavy lifting, while your client remains unmoved.

By asking for their willingness, you suggest a deep respect for their wishes. You also imply their active involvement in the healing process.

I once had an employee assistance program (EAP) client who came for therapy due to a recent traumatic incident at his workplace. As the initial conversation evolved, it triggered an older memory of abuse when he was a teenager. Having framed his traumatic memory of his younger days as a problem that is affecting him, I said I could help him. Then I asked, "Are you willing to work on this here in therapy?" He said, "No. Not really. I can see that this stems from my earlier experience, but I don't think I can face it right now."

My task was first to respect his wishes, and then to "re-frame" it. "What do you think we should focus on that will not push you over the limit, but would still be important for you to work on at this point?" He said, "Maybe just to deal with this current incident... And some tips on how to cope with my daily life. I don't want this to affect my life at home, with my wife and kids." So I said, "Your wife and children mean the world to you, and this is going to drive you to find ways to deal with all of this stuff that is surfacing." It was at this point that I had a buy-in.

Knock before you enter, and know which doors to close (for now).

See also 15. Figure Out Your Client's Circle of Development, 20. The Goal May be to Figure Out the Goal, 22. Frame It.

24. FOLLOW THE PAIN

"The truth will set you free... But first it will hurt like hell."
~ *First heard from a friend, Edwyn de Souza. Original source*
unknown.

The term "follow the pain" is borrowed from Leslie Greenberg's work in emotion-focused therapy. He and co-author Jeanne Watson call it "developing a pain compass," using it as an emotional tracking device.[1] Bruce Ecker, lead proponent of coherence therapy, says that once you find the pain spot, "Pitch a tent. Set up camp right there."[2]

This is a distinctive feature in psychotherapy. It goes where no hairdresser, bartender, or even well-meaning family and friends would go. When others hear something painful, their instinctive reaction is to soothe or divert to another topic.

In the task of therapy, we are not to soothe too quickly, but rather to make room and deepen the experience of the complex layer of emotions. We needn't be cold-hearted in the process, as we need to offer a healing presence as we "follow the pain." This can be done in many ways without prematurely "bandaging it up," such as providing empathic reflections, or even disclosing your emotional reactions. Implicitly, this can be done by slowing down the pace, lowering and deepening your voice, leaning forward to communicate presence and attentiveness.

When we soothe too quickly, we shut the door. Especially in the first session, we want to welcome our client's emotional world, as their inner life doesn't get invited into their usual social realm often.

There is a fine line between trauma and healing. We "follow the pain" because we facilitate its healing.

See also **4. Avoid TBU ("True But Useless") Information, 21. Define the Lead Story, 25. Follow the Spark.**

25. FOLLOW THE SPARK

"Find a place inside where there's joy,
and the joy will burn out the pain."
~ Joseph Campbell, mythologist, writer.

We can't just follow the pain. We also need to "follow the spark."

"What peaks your interest? What do you like doing? What do you do for fun?"

These aren't ice-breaker questions. They are fire-starters. Figure what your clients enjoy devoting their time and attention to, is quintessential in the first session. Weave your interventions using your client's sparks. You want their sparks to catch their problems on fire.

I learned this lesson early on when I was doing my post-graduate practicum in a secondary school. The teachers must have mistaken me for a discipline master, as they would send me kids who were acting up. One morning, as soon as I showed up, the school principal came to me and said that she was sending Jonah to see me in the next period—which was in five minutes. Before she left, she said, "By the way, just so that you are prepared, he punched the last counsellor at the family service agency."

"What? What happened?"

"He said he didn't like the look on his face."

I was left with two minutes before the school bell rang for the next period, and I was in panic mode. Before I could start to think clearly, Jonah arrived at the office. He was big for a 15-year-old.

"Hello. I am Daryl."

"What's this about?" he asked.

I said, "Wanna go for a drink at the canteen?"

He looked more suspicious.

"I'm paying," I said. We walked to the canteen.

What ensued changed everything. I said, "I know that I'm a psychologist, and I'm supposed to ask you all these questions about your problems. The truth is, I'm more interested to know what you do for fun. What sort of interests do you have?"

He sized me up and said, "You wouldn't know anything about it."

"Try me."

He said, "I play the sitar." He paused, waiting for my response.

"That is so cool! Are you serious? I play the sitar too."

"Yeah right. No way... You're kidding right?"

The rest is history. In the sessions after, I gravitated towards the use of music metaphors (rhythm, harmony, melody) and how these applied to his presenting concerns of impulse control and anger management ("Letting the notes breathe between the notes," for emotion regulation, "paying attention to others rather than focus on the self," for fostering prosocial behaviour). In one of our sessions, we cut the talk and had a musical jam! (I'm sure if my practicum supervisor found out, she wouldn't have approved of it as "evidenced-based practice").

Of course, not every client will have the same interests as you, though it certainly helps if you have a broad palette for things in life. In the early session, the key is to be able to tap into what the late Klause Grawe calls "resource activation." He and his colleague Daniel Gassman found that eliciting problems alone did not predict good outcomes. The researchers noted, "Unsuccessful therapists focussed more on the patient's problems and tended to overlook the patient's resources." Instead, the degree of resource activation distinguished successful sessions from the unsuccessful sessions.[1]

Sometimes, all it takes is to ask, "What's important for you in your life right now?" Don't rush your clients for an answer. Tell them you are not looking for the *right* answer, but one that is *real* and alive for them. Renowned journalist Cal Fussman who has interviewed several icons like Mikhail Gorbachev, Jimmy Carter, Muhammad Ali, recommends that the best strategy to get to the heart of an interview is to "find out what they love."[2] Remember: EVERYONE wants to tell their story, not just about their symptoms.

A client in his 40s told me "I just want to be there for *my people* (his family and colleagues)." Even though he was seeing me for the treatment of depressive symptoms, it was clear to me what's meaningful for him. If I didn't follow his spark in his life, no matter how hard I fanned the flame for self-care, it wouldn't ignite the fire. His antidote to his low mood would be to reignite his desire to connect with his wife and kids, and the people he was mentoring at work.

It's not enough to do cheerleading therapy or just "build on strengths." Treat "Follow the Pain" as your left foot, and "Follow the Spark" as your right foot. You need both in order to create movement.

See also 17. How Do You Start a First Session? Reveal Yourself, 21. Define the Lead Story, 24. Follow the Pain.

26. WHAT TO EXPECT

Never assume your clients know what to expect. Expectation influences reality.

W hen my wife and I were expecting our first child, we spoke to a lot of people, and read a lot of books and websites to prepare ourselves. Some were useful, some were actually hilarious, and some were just overwhelming. One book that stood out was *What to Expect When You are Expecting.*[1] The book (there's an app for this too) provides a week-by-week account of every stage of pregnancy, from preconception to postpartum.

The *What to Expect* book does well in giving expecting parents a clear look-ahead. Likewise, at the start of therapy, it is useful to orient your client, and give them a handle on what's installed for this session and what to expect down the road.

Cognitive scientist, Carmen Simon shares a question she is often asked, "'If I tell others what will happen during an upcoming conversation, meeting, or presentation, won't that spoil it?' Receiving ample information ahead of time is not a letdown. This is because the *proof* of what will happen influences people's feeling of power."

On the flip side, having ambiguous information ahead of time will lead to a sense of disempowerment.[2]

In the first session of therapy, we cannot assume our clients know what to expect. As a guide, there are three key areas to cover with your clients: Your role as a therapist, the role of your client, and raising expectations in the process of therapy (see the next three chapters).

See also **27. The Role of Therapist, 28. The Role of Client, 29. Raising Expectations.**

27. THE ROLE OF THERAPIST

Ask your client, "What role do you see me playing in our work together?"

Sounds simple, doesn't it? I would be the first to admit that this question still slips my mind.

Once a client said to me, "I want you to fix of all of my problems... make them go away." (Fantasising) Other times, I hear something like, "At the end of the day, I need to sort this out on my own," (rigidity about independence) or "Can you help my husband to change?" (externalising the location of change). And most often I hear this: "I don't know."

Many metaphors can be ascribed to the function of a psychotherapist. A co-journeyer, listening ear, coach, agent of change, conduit, nurturer, confessor, etc.

Figure out how your client sees your role in the treatment process. Even if they have no idea, be prepared to propose a cogent metaphor. Borrowing from Robert Francher's idea of an "auxiliary mind",[1] I'd say to my clients, "You know, it takes two to know one...Suffering is wasted when we suffer alone... I hope I can provide another mind for you to think out loud together, and help you work through your challenges." Or if appropriate, I might use a coaching metaphor, "Think about it for a little while. Why is it that it's ok for sportsmen to have coaches to help them get better, and why is it taboo for you and I to have a little guidance to get better in our lives?"

See also **26. What to Expect, 28. The Role of Client, 29. Raising Expectations.**

28. THE ROLE OF CLIENT

Don't assume your clients know what they need to do to become an active agent of change. I once asked a client in his fifties this question, "I don't want to make some misguided assumptions, but how do you see your role in our sessions together?" He replied, "That's ok. I'm not so sure either... but all I know is that 'assumption' makes an ass of you and me."

If you think about it, it's a hard question for clients to answer. What I recommend is—with a consideration how you typically work in therapy—you propose to your clients how you might work in the sessions, and be prepared to do course-correction if they do not sit well with your initial ideas.

For example, regarding in-session activities, I might propose: "In order for you to reap the optimal level of benefit from these sessions, we may do some exercises in the sessions. Most people don't need an interpretation of things. Rather, they need a new experience to help them grow. Does that sit well with you?"

Regarding between-session activities, I might address the topic of therapy assignments/tasks/homework/experiments. "In order for you to reap the maximal level of benefit from these sessions, I will be giving you some tasks to do in between our visits. It might be reading resources, specific points to reflect on, journaling, or some form of behavioural experiments. Are you willing?"[1]

Though talk is the lifeblood of therapy, I want to move beyond talk, and hint at a *call for action*. In other words, my spiel on between-session activities is meant to serve as a bridge, crossing from relational talking to behavioral change.

Invite your clients to become an active agent of their change process.
Therapy is not done unto them, but *with* them.

If your in-session and between-session expectations of your clients are different from mine, make it clear to yourself. Then find a way to convey your treatment rationality and how it will benefit your clients.

See also **26. What to Expect, 27. The Role of Therapist, 29. Raising Expectation, 39. Call to Action.**

29. RAISING EXPECTATIONS

Try asking your clients this simple question in the first session: "In terms of a percentage (0% to 100%), How much do you think you would improve by the end of the treatment period?"[1]

Michael Constantino and his team highlighted the following:

If we can influence a person's expectation of therapy, we stand a chance of increasing engagement and the likelihood of a good outcome.[2]

For instance, if a client rates low in their initial treatment expectation, I would recommend that you address their ideas around therapy, past experiences with seeking help, and if there are any blocking beliefs or myths surrounding the notion of therapy.

While you may not be able to give a blow-by-blow account of what to expect, what you can provide your clients is a sense of the following:

1. Explicate both your role and your client's in the process of therapy (see the previous chapters);
2. How frequent you suggest meeting up in the initial stage,[3] and
3. While you will continue to be supportive of them, tell your clients to expect some struggles as you work through difficult issues with them, slightly nudging them out of their comfort zone.

See also 15. **Figure Out Your Client's Circle of Development, 26. What to Expect, 27. The Role of Therapist, 28, The Role of Client.**

30. SWEET ANTICIPATION

Much of the anticipation gets built up even before the first session. By providing an induction into therapy, you not only manage, but optimise expectations. This creates a sense of predictability, and predictability establishes a sense of control. A typical pop/rock/folk song has a sense of predictability; the arch of a song moves from *verse, chorus, verse, chorus, bridge, chorus.*

You want to go one step further.

In your first session, you want to create *predictability* and introduce novelty.

Back to neuroscientist Carmen Simon: "We're dealing with a paradox: on one hand, we want to help people predict our communication accurately, but on the other, we want to provide novelty to trigger a larger spike in dopamine (a pleasure-reward neurotransmitter)."[1]

A good way to blend this predictability-novelty mix is to start with the familiar. Start with the safe topics. Then orient your client on what to expect in this first meeting (and maybe even

provide a hint on what to expect in the subsequent sessions if he
or she so decides to embark on this journey with you). Finally,
make a case for why therapy is a different kind of talk, compared
to talking with their hairdresser (create predictability). Often, the
main aim of therapy is to help your client stretch out of their
comfort zone and grow as they face their difficulties. By saying
something like this, I provide anticipation. I would add that I
want them not only to treat this room as a personal sacred space,
but for the next hour or so, "I will provide guidance of the
process, and I may offer some suggestions of feedback along the
way." (Introduce novelty).

The arc of a good session follows a similar trajectory to a good
story or presentation. This usually starts with the familiar; then a
new component is introduced, allowing greater familiarity to
settle in with some repetition, and then moves on to other new
material.

Watch any good improv actor or jazz musician in action. They
make it seem like they are making stuff out of thin air, but if you
look carefully, you'll notice they are usually paying close attention *and* looking ahead. Just one or two steps ahead. After all,
improvisation originates from the Latin *improvisus*, meaning "not
yet seen ahead of time." We can't see ahead of time within the
process of therapy, but we can co-create a melody to move in
sweet anticipation from the first session to the next.

People don't need a new explanation; they need a **new experience.** Your task is to provide a taste of that in their interaction
with you in the first session, and how that can permeate into
future sessions and their lives outside of the therapy room.

See also **29. Raising Expectations, 31. Exercising Restraint: Tag It,
56. Why Do You Need to Score Your First Sessions? 57. How Do
You Close A First Session?**

31. EXERCISING RESTRAINT: TAG IT

"All the art of living lies in a fine mingling of letting go and holding on." ~Havelock Ellis

In Barry Schwartz's classic book, *The Paradox of Choice*, he shares a study conducted by psychologists Sheena Iyengar and Mark Lepper, which found that consumers were 10 times more likely to purchase jam on display when the number of jams available was reduced from 24 to 6. A more recent meta-analysis combed 99 such studies on choice overload, and the findings hold true.[1] Fewer options make it easier for one to choose. Too much choice overwhelms. Fewer jam options led to better sales.

What does this mean for your first session? Ration your ideas. Exercise restraint. Create a column in your case notes called **Tags.** List a handful of ideas that you want to revisit.

Why should we write down these tags?

1. I scribble these down in the session so I can tamper the voice inside my head and listen to what my client is actually saying.

2. Has it ever happened to you when you have an idea you think it's so good that you are not going to forget it...And eventually, you can't recall what it was? Enter foresight bias.[2] Pen it down.

3. By having written down as a tag, it helps you resist the urge to cover that point, right at that very moment. This prevents you from recency bias.

4. Having a handful of these ideas un-weds you from "the one" idea. This, in turn, makes you more flexible, open and curious to listen to your client.

5. By the end of the first session, quickly go through your tag list. Present one suggestion/intervention/reflection that is in line with your client's top priority. Some call this a treatment plan. Remember to check-in with your client about how they are receiving this piece of feedback from you.

Resist the urge to review all of the tags at the end of the first session. Let the rest of the ideas in your tags be possible building blocks for future sessions. You may choose to share some of these as possible areas to explore next time. This is crucial, because it sends the signal that you are looking ahead. This fosters a sense of hope and expectancy for the treatment process.[3]

Prevent yourself from becoming a therapist who rattles from one idea to the next without pause and awareness that the other person has become overwhelmed. By exercising restraint, you develop an effective focus.

See also **3. The 4Ps versus the 1P; 11. Gifting: Give a Gift, 30. Sweet Anticipation.**

32. ASK "WHO?"

A person is a being and a belonging.
Know who they feel belonged to.

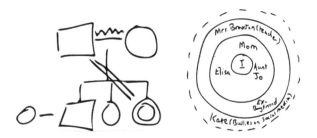

Paint the constellation of people in the person's life. Use diagrams like genograms and sociograms to help you and your clients concretely visualise them. It also helps that you have a record of the significant people in your client's life. Find out how relationships mean to them.

An almost surefire way to get teens talking in the first session is to talk about their friends. Who's who, who they hang out with, who they fall in love with (Ask who they shared their *first kiss* with) and who broke their heart. Ask them who annoys them and why. This is a powerful way to energise a conversation.

Ask the names of key individuals. It's better to refer to "Loretta" than to say, "your wife." If someone talks about their grandfather, find out what he calls him in their cultural context.[1] When you use names, you add an emotional resonance to the conversation. You might have trouble remembering all the names, so write them down.

There are three universal guides for a systemic enquiry:

1. Life: Figure out who impacted the client's Life;
2. Love: Who they fell in Love with/who Loved them (Fred Rogers would say, "Who has loved you into being?"[2]), and
3. Loss: who they've Lost, and their experience of loss, and how it has impacted them.

You may not find out all about the 3Ls in the first session, but you certainly want to have them in your mind as you join the dots of key relationships in their lives.

See also **24. Follow the Pain, 25. Follow the Spark.**

33. PAST ATTEMPTED SOLUTIONS

The psychodynamic camp says, "Your past is the problem." The third wave mindfulness therapist says "Mindlessness is the problem." The emotion-focused therapist says, "Your unresolved feelings are the problem." The pioneering team at Mental Research Institute (MRI), Palo Alto says "the attempted solution is the problem." The solution-oriented practitioner says "There are exceptions to the problem." Meanwhile, the problem-solving camp says "There are solutions to the problems," and the narrative therapist says, "The person is not the problem, the problem is the problem."

PAST ATTEMPTS TO RESOLVE THE ISSUE

Whatever your frame of thinking is, in the first session, you need to figure out your client's past attempts to resolve the issue that they've come to you for help.

Here are some examples:

1. A depressed and anxious teen tells you that she copes by

playing computer games on her mobile device (distraction).

2. A 42-year-old client reveals that he binge-eats when he experiences a setback (self-soothing).

3. A newly wedded lady says that she calls her mother whenever she is feeling blue and disengages with her husband, though there isn't any problem in the marital relationship (difficulty in life-transition and individuation).

4. A 28-year-old aspiring writer finds it hard to get started and procrastinates getting any writing done for a long time (self-critical and perfectionism).

What you want to do next is help the client evaluate the short- and long-term effectiveness of their attempted solutions.

Remember, more than likely, if their attempted solutions worked, they wouldn't be seeing you.

Next, figure out if their attempted solutions fuel the problem. If so, even if it may be obvious, help your clients see the link.

Then you can offer some alternatives. Here's some based on the same examples above:

1. I might suggest for her to connect with a close friend (over the phone or face-to-face) when she is feeling down.

2. I might help this client to "slow it down," delay the immediate binge-eating, and start the process of learning to "befriend emotions" at later sessions.

3. I might ask this newly wedded couple to set aside a weekly ritual to "date" her workaholic husband. Eat out and chat. And every evening, I would suggest a mobile

device ban two hours before bedtime. The intention is to promote "boredom" and opportunities for emotional and physical intimacy.

4. I might suggest for the writer to create stages in his writing. The first stage is a free-form, "for my own eyes only" draft. The second stage is "for the reader," that is, he will edit to make it easier for the reader. Finally, at the third stage, in honor of his self-critique, he would need to switch on that harsh voice, which previously got him stuck at this initial stage of writing. This final stage is called"for the critics."[1]

The possibilities are endless when you shine a light on the specifics of your client's past attempted solutions.

PAST PROFESSIONAL HELP

Another important aspect of your client's past is to note if your client has sought help before. If so, find out what their experience of therapy was like. Ask, "What was helpful?" Then ask, "What was unhelpful?" Ask for specifics, and share your reasons for asking. "The reason I'm asking you this is not to gossip. It's so that I can learn from your past experience, do more of what helped you, and stay clear of making those mistakes—even minor ones —that happened in your previous therapy."

For example, if a client says that she didn't like the fact that she just "talked and talked" and didn't get anything out of the session, this hints that you might want to be more proactive with this client. If another client says that she stopped after the second session because she felt like she was being interrogated, you might want to be sensitised to the way you ask questions, and not bombard her with clinical checklists types of questions.

Finally, if your client says, "All's good. No issue," but yet still made the change of therapist to come and see you, if there were no other extraneous issues, note that this client possibly finds it overwhelming to share her feelings. In this case, you can note this, and observe whether there is a pattern of her struggling with revealing her feelings to you (i.e., she might start to get anxious in the session talking about her feelings). If so, at an appropriate time in the first session, name the elephant in the room. "I can imagine it must be hard to give voice to your feelings. In fact, you might even feel too vulnerable to share it with another person... with me. Just to check, how intense was today for you, on a scale of one to ten?" (Client responds with an eight to nine.) "Wow. So this leaves you feeling really raw today. You might be wondering how I see you after you shared about yourself. I want to say how much I respect your courage and effort for doing this, for coming here, and sharing a part of you with me today. You know, in the future sessions, if there's a topic that's too overwhelming for you, you have every right to say to me 'I'm not ready to discuss that,' and I'd fully respect that."

After you've done that, check in again. "Do you mind if I ask, how similar or different is today's first session for you compared with your previous experience of therapy?" How she replies here is going to teach you a whole lot. Take verbatim notes of what your clients say.

By learning about your clients' past attempts to resolve their problems and their past professional help, you can provide a *difference* that is of value.

See also 19. "What is Your View of the Problem?", 31. Exercising Restraint: Tag It, 10. Listen in Order to Questions, or Question in Order to Listen.

34. TIMELY QUESTIONS

We conflate timely and timeless matters. Make a distinction between them.

Timely questions are urgent issues.

If someone poses a suicide risk, it's urgent. If someone's ambivalent about being in therapy, it's urgent. If someone's hungry or thirsty in the session, it's urgent. If someone is anxious in the session, it's urgent. Even though something's urgent, we shouldn't panic. Instead, we simply prioritise.

If there is a suicide risk, you need to assess and sort out a safety plan. We not only need to assess risk, but also organising resources available to help the person, and touching deeply on their life-giving factors.[1]

Another timely issue may pertain to assessing who's the bearer of the problem. For example, if a youth was asked by his mother to come for the session, even though he doesn't see an issue, it would be a timely concern to make sure that you get the mother's perspective as soon as possible. This could be from the horse's mouth, or you could ask the client to relate from his mother's perspective.

When someone's highly anxious, you need to ask questions about their level of anxiety in the moment. For example, you'd ask, "As this is your first time here in my office, before we go further, what are you feeling right now?"

"I'm a bit nervous, to be honest... I don't know what to expect."

"Right. I really appreciate you saying that. We will talk about what to expect from therapy in a minute. But for now, do you know where you feel the nervousness in your body?" (The client takes a moment. She takes a deep breath.)

"I notice my heart beating faster than usual... and my stomach's like a knot at the moment..."

"This is a good start that you can notice these signals of anxiety. Let's take some time to just be with those physical sensations, make room and attend to what arises as we take the next few steps..."

Other times, timely issues may even pertain to tangential issues. I once had a client who worked as a manual laborer. He came from overseas to work. He had to deal with some family issues during his holiday back in his home country. Unbeknownst to me at first, his boss had accompanied him to the clinic and was waiting outside. During the session, I picked up his hesitant look, as if he was repeatedly saying, "Yes, but..." to most of my statement. So I broached the question, "We are about to end the session, but I feel like I'm missing something. Can you help me explain this?" And he said, "Actually, can you provide a letter to explain to my boss about why I'm having difficulties with focusing at work due to what's happening in my family overseas?" That was all he wanted. In fact, he said he wasn't keen on therapy, and just needed to sort it out on his own. I gave him the letter, and with his permission, decided to speak with his boss briefly. He was relieved that his boss was more understanding than he expected.

A month later, he rang our clinic and decided to schedule an appointment to see me on his own accord. Now, he wanted therapy.

TIMELY QUESTIONS TO ASK:

What has been on your mind?
What's a pressing issue for you?
What hurts the most?
What are you feeling right now in your body?

See also **3. The 4Ps vs. the 1P, 13. Assessing Risks from Both Sides, 24. Follow the Pain, 25. Follow the Spark, 35. Timeless Questions, 36. Timely and Timeless Questions?**

35. TIMELESS QUESTIONS

If timely questions are about urgent matters, timeless questions are about the perennials. It's about what's most important.

If we fail to make a distinction between urgent and important matters, urgency will win every time.

Urgent matters can be important, but often, there's usually a large untapped fraction that is important and not urgent.

I saw Alfred, a 52-year-old who suffered a stroke and then a heart attack on separate occasions. He was an unrelenting workaholic and a self-admitted shrewd businessman. The illness stopped him on his tracks, and he was sinking into depression. I said to him, "You know, you spent all your adult life working so damn hard to build your business. You gave it your blood, sweat and tears. Heck, you nearly gave your life and sold your soul for it. But let's stop for a second. Alfred, what's *really* important to you? What do you want your life to stand for?"

Alfred fell back into his chair. He began to weep. "I don't know. I don't know." He went to say that for a long time, he rarely afforded himself the time to stop and reflect on where he was going. We began our work on looking deep into what really mattered to him, and helping him to re-evaluate his life, and channeling his energy on things that are vital. In the subsequent session, we began to talk about what a "terrible gift" his illness has been to him. It nearly killed him, and it woke him up.

TIMELESS QUESTIONS TO ASK:

If we take a step back and see from the eyes of your future self, what do you want to contribute to in this life?
What does a really good day look like to you?[1]
Who's an important person in your life? What makes this relationship special to you?
When were the darkest times you've experienced? How did you overcome it?

See also 3. The 4Ps vs. the 1P, 24. Follow the Pain, 25. Follow the Spark, 34. Timely Questions, 36. Timely and Timeless Questions?

36. TIMELY AND TIMELESS QUESTIONS?

There is a small portion in the middle that timely and timeless questions co-exist. For example, when someone comes in with suicide risk, it's important to not only try and manage the person's safety (i.e., urgent issue), but also to make room to delve deeper as the person is tormented by "psychache"[1](i.e., important issue).

When faced with a crisis, anxious therapists often circumvent going deeper into the sea of pain. But the discerning therapist knows that she needs to touch on the wound that manifests itself in the client's contemplations of cutting off life, as an attempt to cut off the pain.

The ancient Greeks have two words for time: *Chronos* and *kairos*. The former refers to chronological time, while the latter refers to a critical and opportune moment, or sometimes referred to as the *eternal now* or *deep time*— that is, "past, present, and future all at once."[2]

Perhaps the intersection between what's timely and timeless is to step beyond *chronological time* and into *deep time*.

TIMELY-TIMELESS QUESTIONS TO ASK:

To a client who is at risk of suicide: Shall we find a way to end your problems, not your life?[3]
Let's take the time in today's session to make room and slow it down...Tell me, what has happened to you?
What has your inner life been like?

(Note: See also the questions in chapters Timely Questions and Timeless Questions.)

See also 3. The 4Ps vs. the 1P, 24. Follow the Pain, 25. Follow the Spark, 34. Timely Questions, 35. Timeless Questions.

37. HEALING QUESTIONS

I learned the powerful lesson of healing questions from the receiving end. One time in my life, I was a complete mess. Thankfully, I was in the good hands of a therapist who understood the profound impact of asking not just the right questions, but also using questions that heal.

I remember more the feeling than the actual words that my therapist used in our first session. But I was cognisant enough to note the impact her questions had on me. I was keen to invoke such a powerful feeling in others in my work as a therapist.

Here are snippets of what my therapist asked me:

"How do you keep the life-giving spirit alive in spite of the ongoing struggles?"

"What does it mean to you that you are just trying to do the right thing?"

"Where did you learn to be others-centered and not self-centered in your approach to life?"

"What does that say about you as a person?"

The magic was not in her words; it also wasn't in the way she said it, though she was bent forward, unhurried and soft. I didn't have the answers to her questions at that time, but that wasn't the point. The important point was *what I said to myself* based on the questions she asked.[1] She lit a spark in me.

The effect of those healing questions created a sense of meaning and personal agency... And these were all experienced in the first session!

It was later that I learned about asking questions that trigger "self-reflexivity," which promotes internalising of our ability and resources.[2]

I recently heard an interview with the 87-year-old renowned radio and television host, Larry King. He was asked about how he used questions. He said, "Nobody thinks of himself as a bad person....If I were to interview Osama Bin Laden, the stupidest first question would be, 'Why did you kill 3,000 people on that September day in New York?' I would have asked him, 'You grew up in the richest family in Saudi Arabia... *Why did you leave?*'"[3] Such a question is more likely to help the interviewee open up, even if the person's a terrorist.

If you use it thoughtfully, questions have the power to heal.

See also **10. isten in Order to Question, or Question in Order to Listen? 25. Follow the Spark.**

38. DON'T JUST EMPATHISE;
SAY IT.

The foundation of the counselling and psychotherapy profession rests on one key ingredient: empathy. Yet empathy is often a tool that is blunted by too much talking about it, instead of being sharpened by the act of *expression*.

We often mistake *feeling* empathy for explicitly communicating empathy to our clients. Like us, our clients can't read minds.

Explicate your empathy and respect for your client. Learn to articulate it with words that come out of your mouth.

Michael Fishman points out the importance of communicating in copywriting what a person "Will say, won't say, and can't say."[1] In therapy, what a person *will say* is often the obvious presenting problems or symptoms. What a person *won't say* is what's implicit in their suffering. Finally, what the person *can't say* relates to vulnerable elements of themselves, relating to the core—and often painful—self-narratives. The latter sometimes is a blind spot.

Here are some examples of how I've adapted Fishman's idea and how you can communicate empathy in therapy, using the *Will Say, Won't Say, Can't Say as a* mental model:

"You know, when you were talking about the need to accomplish so much in your work and family life (*will say*), I can't help but sense an overwhelming anxiety in you... pushing yourself harder and harder each time...(*won't say*). It's like, you worry that you will let them down and be this tragic failure to your family (*can't say*)."

"You are not only angry at your partner for ignoring you (will say), you are also hurt by his lack of understanding the loneliness that you are experiencing (won't say)... You are left wondering 'Is there something wrong with me? Am I not good enough? (can't say)'"

"What you are saying is, you've not only lost someone you love (will say), but you've also lost a part of yourself (won't say)... And there's a part that is left feels alone and abandoned (can't say). Does that sound right?"

Other times, you might want to simply honor your client and say, "Edward, I want you to know that I've deep respects for you and what you are doing to improve your life."

A related point: When we express empathy toward our clients, do not seek to be right about your empathic conjectures. Seek to reach out. Be willing to be corrected, if you didn't quite get it right.

See also 10. Listen in Order to Question, or Question in Order to Listen? 19. "What is Your View of the Problem? 40. Be A "Withness."

39. CALL TO ACTION

Teachers and coaches do this one thing well. They call it homework.

While therapy is not a classroom lesson or a game of shooting hoops, we can glean learnings outside the therapy room. After all, we want to maximise the impact of a session and influence the client's prospective memory of the session in a compelling way.

If you take this idea of a "call to action" seriously, at the end of the first session, you'd be conveying confidence that therapy is not just talk, but it is about creating a climate of change in their lives. The combination of in-session and between-session activities is more likely to create change, as opposed to the influence of in-session activities only.[1]

Some therapists are not comfortable being prescriptive. While we may not be prescribing pharmaceuticals, we can certainly suggest possible behavioural strategies. Being able to recommend or at least address this subject at the end of the first session implicitly conveys confidence in your approach.

Here are some examples of between-session activities you can prescribe.

AN EXPERIMENT

Here are some examples of what an experiment would look like.

To a socially anxious person: "I would like you to run your own social experiment. For the next week, I would like you to be curious. Keenly observe what stories pass through your mind when you are just about to be in a social situation. Note them down on your phone."

To a self-critical client: "I want you to read this card that I've written for you (It says "Act First, Think Later"). This is quite contrary to what we've been taught to do in school, isn't it? We were told to think before we act. Let's try this out. For the next week before we meet again, I want you to try this on for size. I would like you to suspend your evaluations, and just act upon what you need to do for your job hunt first. Then *after* the fact, I would like you to ruminate your heart out. Remember, do this after, not before. How does that sound?"

When you frame the task as an experiment, you communicate to your client that their *experience*, not your explanation, matters the most. You're asking them to find out for themselves.

AN ATTENTIONAL FOCUS

"What's ONE thing that you want to remember from today? How are you going to hold this idea with you through to next week?" (My intentions: To influence their retrieval cues and future recall).

You can help your client's attentional focus by writing down a key sentence or word on an index card to keep in their wallet or pocket. This compacted phrase chunks the gist, not the details, of the first session.

A REFLECTION

Here's an exercise: "I would like you to take some time after this session to go back and journal (Draw, write a poem, or a song) about what led you to this point in your life."

Alternatively, here's an exercise that can be done interpersonally: "After today's session, I would like you to give your best friend Rebecca a call. Ask her if she can spare you five to ten minutes. Ask her to give you some honest feedback on how she sees you. If she's wondering why this question came out of the blue, say that this is what your odd-ball therapist who you've just met, asked you to do. After your chat with Rebecca, take some time to reflect on what she said about you."

The point of a reflection is to influence the future. While it may seem like it's a retrospective "thinking about the past" idea, the intention of a reflective assignment is to create a space for taking stock of a person's life, so that he can design a better future.

A HOMEWORK

For those who weren't traumatised by their school teachers, I might prescribe some homework. I might say read a book, article, task, do an exercise, etc.

Maybe it's a reflection of my own bias, but I rarely see an individual who likes homework. The only time I prescribe "homework" is when a highly motivated client is asking me, "So what can I do between now and the next time we meet?"

I keep an archive in a note taking application in Evernote called, "Client Resources." In there, I clip web pages, articles, book recommendations that I think might be useful for clients. Later, I might share them with my clients as reading materials for those who are information hungry.

SELF-PRESCRIPTION

"Based on what we've talked about today, what do you feel *compelled* to do? What's something you can take action on between now and the next time we meet?"

Whenever possible, I prefer to ask clients to self-prescribe what they want to do as a call to action. People are more persuaded by their own logic. Usually, it helps the job along when there's a natural flow from the highlighted problem to an untapped individual or interpersonal resource. For example, for a client who has been isolated for some time due to his fears of evaluation from others, I might emphasise how tired he is of letting fear take over his life, and then I'd follow-up with the above question, "What do you feel compelled to do at this critical point in your life right now?"

A "call to action" creates a climate of change and invokes therapeutic engagement outside of therapy.

Help your clients act upon what was seeded in words.

See also 11. **Gifting: Give a Gift, 28. The Role of Client, 41. How Do You Close a First Session?**

40. BE A "WITH-NESS"

"Rather than focusing on creating things, I am learning more to appreciate simply being a witness to simple beauty in life... like the clouds."~ Iggy Pop, at age 68.

Every now and then, you will be blessed with a situation where your client has done all the work, even before he or she begins the work with you. Don't mess this up.

When this comes knocking at your door, don't just witness it; be a part of it. Be a "With-ness."[1]

Listen to their stories. Listen to their courage to heal, and how they rise above adversities and oppositions. Witness their metamorphosis not from afar, but be with them through the journey. "With-ness" communicates to the person, *"I am there for you every step of the way. I am with you. I honor you."*

Once 19-year-old male came to the first session with his mother. His GP referred him to me because he was diagnosed with major depression, and he had attempted suicide about a month before. Both of them looked solemn. I introduced myself and my setup, and got them to fill in the outcome rating scale (ORS)[2], a measure of the person's wellbeing. His mother filled the ORS from her perspective as a parent. I was prepared for his scores to be higher than his mother's, as I assumed that he was the "unwilling" party at this initial meeting. His scores reflected that he was doing just fine (i.e., in the non-clinical range), while his mother's caregiver ratings suggested a much lower score (i.e., in the clinical range). I would never have guessed what he said to me when I enquired about the high scores. First, I asked him if he would have scored the same three to four weeks back. He said no, "it would have been much lower."

"What caused things to pick up?"

"I woke up."

"When?"

"After I jumped."

"What do you mean?"

"I didn't realise how much pain I put my family through. It only dawned on me when we were at the hospital. I saw the look in my mom's eyes, and then my siblings. I went, 'Oh my goodness. What have I done?' I can't f*%k this up again."

At this point, both mother and son were in tears. Our work began not with sorting out his depression, but it became the stage for setting up the rite of passage of self-forgiveness, followed by reconciliation with his family members.

My role for him and his family was to actively be a "with-ness," standing in awe of our humanity, as he began to breathe life back into his life.

See also 22. Frame It, 38. Don't Just Empathise; Say It, 44. The Use of Routine Outcome Monitoring.

41. HOW DO YOU CLOSE A FIRST SESSION?

At the end of a television series, some leave you wanting more. Others frustrate the viewer by ending on a cliffhanger ("To find out what happens, see the next episode..."). Don't do this to your client.

It turns out that when we look back at an experience, we do not recall the entire experience. Instead, our memory is biased towards remembering two moments: The peak and the end.

Daniel Kahneman and his colleagues put this to the test.[1] In one of their studies, they examined patients who were undergoing colonoscopy. Half the group was randomly assigned to a typical treatment group, while the other half were given three extra minutes at the end, with the tip of the colonoscope rest in the rectum. Not exactly a pleasant experience! The results were striking. As the second group experienced less pain at the end—though it was extended by three minutes—patients who underwent the longer procedure actually rated the whole experience as less painful, less unpleasant and less aversive.

The implications of the peak-end rule are simple, yet profound.

Often we evaluate the quality of a movie, meal, and a vacation, not by the entire experience, but by certain moments, especially the way it ended.[2] Pay attention to how you close a session. How we close the first session can be the imprint of how your client remembers you later on.

In the closing few minutes, think about how to create an impact.

How are you going to create an emotional impact on your client? Do not excuse yourself with "reasonableness." *"But this is only the first session..."*

Do not close with administrative matters. It's not the most riveting thing to do. Instead:

- Sum the session up by connecting the dots.
- Give a preview of what's to come.
- Share your reflection and feedback.
- Ask your client, "What's the one thing from this session that struck you the most?"
- Write down one key pointer on a post-it note or an index card for your client to take home.[3]

T.S. Eliot's poem Little Gidding in *Four Quartets* points us in the right direction: "And to make an end is to make a beginning. The end is where we start from."

See also 11. **Gifting: Give a Gift, 30. Sweet Anticipation, 39. Call to Action, 42. Don't Just Ask for Feedback; Give Some.**

42. DON'T JUST ASK FOR FEEDBACK; GIVE SOME.

A psychotherapist in New York once said, "A patient recently told me that, after seeing her therapist for several years, she asked if he had any advice for her. The therapist said, 'See you next week.'"[1]

Therapists often think about how important it is to ask for feedback from our clients, but we often fail to provide the same thing to our clients. By providing our impressions within a therapeutic frame at the end of a first session, we are more likely to co-create with our clients what the poet and philosopher David Whyte calls the "conversational nature of reality."[2] When we provide our experience of the client's reality, a new reality emerges, one that is dialogical, engaged, and alive—not monological, disengaged, and dead. The client is more likely to continue therapy, simply because she has just heard an idea other than her own.

Offer your impressions to the client. Give your perspective. Say what strikes you.

Near the end of the first session, to a highly anxious client who said that it was a huge deal for him coming to the first appointment, I said, "I appreciate you coming here and breaking the silence. Let's continue to give voice to this side of you, and other sides that haven't spoken up just yet."

To a perfectionistic client: "It seems to me that there's a function, a reason why you have learned to be so self-critical. From what you've told me today, it seems like you had to. To get yourself out of the darkness of drugs and bad company. To get yourself together. Because you had no one else to push you or to guide you."

To a teenager who's not telling others the difficulties she's going through inside, I might say, "You know, Vicky, I worry for you."

Client replies, "Why?" She begins to tear. "You don't have to worry about me."

"But I do. In between our sessions, I think about you. Even though you try to show others that you're ok, I worry that no one else sees how much you are really hurting inside."

To a client who's making incremental progress: "Despite the recent struggles you had to face, I noticed you are taking steps out of your comfort zone, and really working on things that are within your control. What's more, I see that you are learning to let go of things that are *not* within your control. What's that like for you? How did you come to this point?"

Avoid the armchair psychology approach. Speak what personally stands out for you. If you don't know where to begin, start by observing what's changed for your client, and open the sentence by saying, "I noticed..."

See also 11. Gifting: Give a Gift, 41. How Do You Close a First Session, 49. Feedback.

43. DEVELOPING A VISUAL OF CLIENT'S OUTCOMES

D on't just say it, show it. Put the progress scores on a spreadsheet, and use a chart wizard.[1] There are now many outcomes software that allow you to digitally score outcome measures like the Outcome Rating Scale and a working alliance measure called the Session Rating Scale[2] Or you can use a pen and draw on a printed graph.

Graphing may not be something you'd do in the first session, but it's worth bringing up in this book because you want to plan to show it from the second session onwards.

Express visually how your client has moved from point A to point B. Even though this is the first session, tell your clients you will be doing so in the subsequent sessions. Tell them *why* you are doing this: "This will give us a chance to monitor our progress, and to see if we are on track or off track. If we are off track, this visual can inform us that I will need to do something different to steer us back on track."

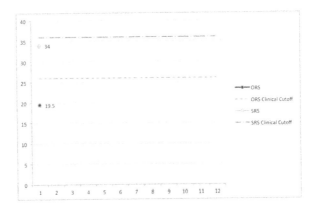

*Baseline scores of the Outcome Rating Scale (ORS) and the
Session Rating Scale (SRS).*

Once you have developed a baseline score, you will now be able
to graph the progress across sessions. Remember, the key is to
make this information visible to both you and your client. Take a
quick check in at every session.

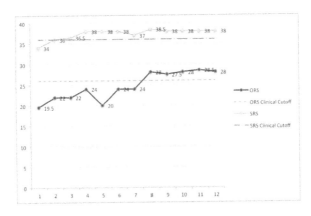

Trajectory of ORS and SRS across subsequent sessions.

Make your client's progress visible to feed the learning process.

Long-term clients especially like getting this longitudinal visual. This snapshot gives them perspective. It also gives therapist perspective. It provides a sense of an unfolding reality with regard to "where we came from," "where we are," and "where we are going."

See also **44. The Use of Routine Outcome Monitoring (ROM), 45. Why Use Formal Feedback. 52. Eliciting Client Feedback.**

SUMMARY OF KEY POINTS TO INCREASING YOUR IMPACT

H ere are the key points to increasing your impact in a first session.

Chapters	Keys to Increasing Your Impact
15. Figure Out Your Client's Circle of Development	Define your client's current comfort zone, learning zone, and panic zone.
16. How Do You Start a First Session? Orient	Orient your client in space and time, so as to set the stage for the work ahead.
17. How Do You Start a First Session? Reveal Yourself	Be vulnerable first.
18. How Do You Start a First Session? Regulate In-the-Moment Anxiety	Help your clients to be fully present. Ask the question, "What is it like for you to be here right now?"
19. "What is Your View of the Problem?"	Do more "perspective getting" than "perspective taking."
20. The Goal May be to Figure Out the Goal	The best goals change *current* actions. And be ready to re-define the goals as things evolve.
21. Define the Lead Story	Figure out the *chorus* (i.e., main theme).
22. Frame It	Move from an old default frame to a new therapeutic frame.
23. Gaining Consensus	Get your client's will on board before going any further.
24. Follow the Pain	Develop a "pain compass" as an emotional tracking device.
25. Follow the Spark	Develop a sense of what ignites your client's life.
26. What to Expect	Never assume your clients know what to expect. Expectation influences reality.
27. The Role of Therapist	Ask your client, "What role do you see me playing in our work together?"
28. The Role of Client	Invite your clients to become an active agent of their change process. Therapy is not done unto them, but *with* them.
29. Raising Expectations	If we can influence a person's expectation of therapy, we stand a chance of increasing engagement and the likelihood of a good outcome.
30. Sweet Anticipation	Create predictability and introduce novelty.
31. Exercising Restraint: Tag It	Hold back your good ideas and ration them appropriately.
32. Ask "Who"	Find out *who* the special people are in your client's life.
33. Past Attempted Solutions	Find out what were your client's past attempted solutions to their current problems.
34. Timely Questions	Define the urgent issues.
35. Timeless Questions	Define what's most important.
36. Timely and Timeless Questions?	Step beyond *chronological time* and into *deep time*.
37. Healing Questions	Use questions to promote a sense of meaning and personal agency.
38. Don't Just Empathise; Say It.	Learn to put your feelings of empathy into words.
39. Call to Action	Transform words into behavioural change.
40. Be A "With-ness"	Learn to *be with* and honor your client's transformation.
41. How Do You Close A First Session?	In the closing few minutes, think about how to create an impact.
42. Don't Just Ask for Feedback, Give Some.	Offer your impressions to the client. Give your perspective. Say what strikes you.
43. Developing a Visual of Client's Outcomes	Make your client's progress visible to feed the learning process.

SECTION III: BUILDING A CULTURE OF LEARNING

Build a culture of learning, and not just performing.

Cultivate this from the first session, in order

to influence the entire process of therapy.

BUILDING A CULTURE OF
LEARNING KEY POINTS

In Section I, the aim is to undo the traditional way of conducting a first session. In Section II, the focus is to create a deeper impact with our clients, so as to sustain engagement.

In this final section, the chapters that follow elaborate on how to cultivate and sustain a vibrant learning environment for therapists' professional development. Though this can be broadly applied beyond the conduct of first sessions, the emphasis on building a culture of learning is crucial, especially if we consider the impact on our clients when they first step into our office. Much of the systems and practices described in the following chapters hinge on how we kick it off at the first session.

We will specifically look at the practical use of routine outcome monitoring in clinical practice, with a framework of deliberate practice to improve your performance, and ways to score the level of vitality in your first sessions.

44. THE USE OF ROUTINE OUTCOME MONITORING (ROM)

M anagement consultant and writer Peter Drucker says, "What gets measured, gets managed."

Measure what is of value to your client. And keep both you and your client's eyes on it.

It's not enough to use measures as a pre- and post-tool. Why? Doing so will put you into a free fall. Practitioners often do this when their agency mandates the use of measures, and no clear clinical utility and integration were emphasised. When measures get used only at the start and end of therapy, it's often just for *evaluative* purposes. The idea behind employing a routine outcome monitoring (ROM) practice is to use it not only for evaluation of service, but also for real-time quality improvement. When we lose sight of the purpose of ROM, we end up valuing what we measure, instead of focusing on measuring what is of value.

ROM = Evaluation + Improving Quality and Effectiveness

What we need to do is use a ROM system that serves you and your clients, session-by-session.

I use the Outcome Rating Scale (ORS) and Session Rating Scale (SRS) at every session. [1] These are ultra-brief measures with four analogue scales and take less than three minutes each to explain (ORS at the beginning, and SRS near the end of the session), and take less than 30 seconds in subsequent sessions.[2] I have been doing so for about a decade now. More recently, I began supplementing the ORS and SRS with another measure, the Clinical Routine Outcome Evaluation-Outcome Measure (CORE-OM),[3] at the start and routine intervals.[4]

Once you start measuring the outcomes and engagement level of each session, you want to integrate the measures into therapy. Do not treat this like some cumbersome administrative matter that is detached from the therapy hour. Why would a GP take your temperature? To check if you are running a fever. Your GP would say, "Yes, your temperature is 39.5 degrees. You are running a fever." She doesn't detach the measurement from clinical care.

We have to weave the measures immediately back to the therapeutic work. How? **Make the measurements visible.** Graph them. Feed the data back to your client and discuss it. When something improves significantly (in the ORS, the reliable change index is 5 points or more), enquire about what they did that impacted this gain. When something dips, ask about it.

A man in his mid-thirties came to seek help for issues relating to OCD and depression. The ORS was administered. As expected, he scored in the clinically distressed range in the ORS and CORE-OM. I explained the scores and I asked him how long had his score been this way. He began to tear, "It's been so many years that I've lost count." This gives me a sense of the protraction of his suffering before seeking help, and this also gets me curious about the impetus that brought him here.

OUTCOMES

When you start measuring outcomes from the first session, down the road, clients will have a relative comparison to make. And it won't be to some abstract normative data, but to their own. Their first session rating is regarded as their **baseline** score. Joseph Campbell would have called this the beginning of the hero's journey. Clients are often surprised by the level of progress when they look back at their initial scores. It offers them perspective of the road they have taken.

Some therapists say the use of measures at the first session gets in the way of engaging with the client. Would we say the same thing when your family doctor takes out his stethoscope to listen to your chest? ROM helps us do our job, rather than get in the way. When you start to use ROM as a **conversation tool**, rather than an assessment tool, you will become more engaged with your clients.

GLOBAL WELL-BEING MEASURES

Why don't I use symptom-specific measures? You can if you choose to, but I only would use a symptom-specific measure as a supplement, not as a primary measure. Even though it is the symptoms that brought them to treatment, clients are more than the sum of their symptoms. A symptom can be reduced in treatment, but the client's life functioning might not necessarily improve. If a client is struggling with auditory hallucinations, he may want to deal with his voice hearing experience, and he may also want to work on getting a job, or to be more connected with people that matter in his life.

People can work on improving their well-being, *in spite* of their symptoms. A symptom-specific measure alone would not be able to reflect this nuance.

See also **43. Developing a Visual of Client's Outcomes, 51. Performance Feedback Versus Learning Feedback, 52. Eliciting Client Feedback.**

45. WHY USE FORMAL FEEDBACK?

There are those who run away from routine outcome monitoring (ROM), and those who embrace it.[1]

On the majority side of the fence, skeptical practitioners are uncomfortable with quantifying their client's wellbeing.

The adamant Non-ROMer might say, "How can a simple outcome measure tell me about whether my client is benefiting from treatment and how effective I am? Besides, change takes a long time to happen, and it's gonna get worse before it gets better."

On the minority side—though growing—these practitioners believe in the importance of tracking outcomes. That said, the rookie ROMer might say, "The outcome measure is sufficient to inform me about whether my client is benefiting from therapy and how effective I am. Change happens early *all* the time, and it *won't* get worse before it gets better."

Like all fundamentalism, such rigid views do not affirm reality.

We cannot farm out decision-making to quantified measures

alone, and neither can we rely solely on intuition, no matter how experienced we may be. Data in and of itself cannot dictate whether one should continue or end treatment, and our intuition is highly susceptible to an overconfidence bias.

To make better clinical judgment, our task is to hold the *tension of opposites*, both in the clinical data and our clinical intuition. In turn, rather than rely solely on borrowed evidence from remote clinical trials that may not represent the clientele we see, we can develop our own native evidence, and use that to hone our intuitive lens.

Data + Intuition = Better Decisions

Contrary to our intuition, here's what we know from psychotherapy outcome studies:

1. Change happens early rather than later, and

2. It doesn't often get worse before it gets better.[2]

This doesn't mean that your client will not experience a delay or a dip in their progress. Life happens. Averages should not negate the individual. But it would be unwise to see the individual and ignore the average base rates.

Here's more of what we know from the cumulative evidence in psychotherapy:

3. We are practically blind when our clients deteriorate in our care,[3] and

4. Differences in therapist skills account for more than treatment models.[4]

Therapists aren't able to accurately spot deterioration due to optimism bias, but it is a relatively straightforward issue to address. Start using formal feedback measures.

It's not so straightforward to improve your performance. For now, it's important to note that an individual client outcome does not tell you how effective you are as a therapist. You would need more than N = 1, 2 or even 3 (at least 20 to 30 closed cases) to make any general conclusion about your effectiveness.[4] Take note: Measurement of outcomes *precede* individualised professional development. A good aggregated baseline of your performance is a pivotal step in your learning and development.

There is science in the arts, and there is art in the sciences. No reason to bifurcate them. Our task is to hold the science and the art, and weave a coherent narrative to create an emotional impact through our work together.

If you buy into this line of reasoning, here's the starting point: begin using formal feedback measures from the FIRST session. This way, you are able to capture a good baseline of your client's wellbeing. If you couple this with an alliance measure from the first session, you get an idea of the level of engagement, right from the get-go.

See also **44. The Use of Routine Outcome Monitoring (ROM), 52. Eliciting Client Feedback.**

46. DELIBERATE PRACTICE

"People make claims about having 20 years' experience, but they really just have one year's experience repeated 20 times."~Educationalist Dylan William.

If you want to take your skills to the next level, incorporate deliberate practice into your profession.

Deliberate practice (DP) is defined as

> "...Individualized training activities especially designed by a coach or teacher to improve specific aspects of an individual's performance through repetition and successive refinement. To receive maximal benefit from feedback, individuals have to monitor their training with full concentration, which is effortful and limits the duration of daily training."[1]

Without a sense of intentional and focused practice, it would be hard to improve on your first sessions in therapy.

Deliberate practice has been found to mediate the development of expert performance in a variety of fields such as music, sports, chess, business, medicine and surgery.[2] Superior performers engage in self-reflection and thinking about their thinking (i.e., meta-cognition) regarding their existing knowledge, while synergistically adopting the mass of knowledge and skill set in order to perform a particular task more efficiently and effectively.[3] Although some performers reach a plateau and begin to disengage from deliberate practice, superior performers are more likely to *counteract automaticity* by developing increasingly complex mental representations to acquire higher levels of control of their performance.[4] In other words, top performers are often pushing beyond their comfort zone to prevent stagnation.

For my doctoral research, I documented the impact of DP in the field of psychotherapy. Specifically, the amount of time spent in solitary focused activities was found to predict client outcomes in a naturalistic setting.[5] In the first eight years of professional work, the top quartile of performers spent, on average, nearly 2.8 times more time deliberately working on improving their skills than the bottom three quartiles. It's hard work to become good at something. Yet, years of experience did not translate to better outcomes. Other therapist characteristics like age, gender, professional qualifications, types of professional and theoretical orientation did not predict differences in therapists' effectiveness.

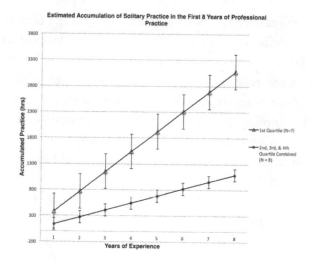

Comparing therapists from the top quartile with the others in the lower quartiles on the basis of their adjusted client outcomes as a function of their accumulative time spent on deliberate practice alone in the first 8 years of clinical practice. Error bars represent standard errors of the mean.

(Source: From Chow, D., Miller, S. D., Seidel, J. A., Kane, R. T., Thornton, J., & Andrews, W. P. (2015). The role of deliberate practice in the development of highly effective psychotherapists. *Psychotherapy, 52*(3), 337-345. doi:http://dx.doi.org/10.1037/pst0000015 *Copyright by American Psychological Association.)*

The key attribute of DP is to "Seek out challenges that go beyond their current level of reliable achievement—ideally in a safe and optimal learning context that allows immediate feedback and gradual refinement by repetition."[6] It is important to note that DP is not only vital for the acquisition of superior performance, but also for skills maintenance.[7] Therefore, in deconstructing the concept of DP and how it applies to improving your first sessions,

I'd break it down into four essential components. In the next four chapters, we will elaborate on each.

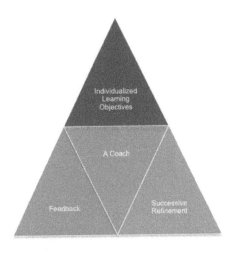

The Four Essential Components of Deliberate Practice[8]

See also **44. The Use of Routine Outcome Monitoring (ROM), 47. Individualised Learning Objectives, 48. A Coach, 49. Feedback, 50. Successive Refinement, 58. Figure Out Your Circle of Development.**

47. INDIVIDUALISED LEARNING OBJECTIVES

Figure out *What* to work on before *How* to get better.

We get lost trying to learn as much as we can, and we often get overwhelmed when our efforts become diffused. Worse still, propagated by our continuous professional development efforts, we end up working on things that have little or no leverage on improving outcomes (e.g., specific techniques and methods, which account for approximately 0-1% of outcomes). Too often, when we engage in clinical supervision on a case-by-case basis, there is often lacking a coherent thread that weaves in the therapist's learning needs with the clinical case concerns.

Relevant to first sessions in therapy, it is vital you ask yourself, *"What is one key aspect of my first sessions that I can be working on, so as to improve my engagement levels with clients?"*

Here are examples of key questions to help you identify what aspects of the first sessions you can work on:

Structure

1. How do you start the session?
2. How do you close a first session?
3. How do you elicit detailed and nuanced feedback?
4. How do you integrate the use of feedback measures into therapy?
5. How do you prepare for a planned closure of therapy?

Hope and Expectancy

1. How do you communicate a hopeful and optimistic stance towards your client? (Generate possibilities)
2. How do you conduct an induction into therapy? (Optimising expectations of therapy; what to expect; role of therapist; role of client; provide an acceptable and adaptive explanation for the client's distress; provide a treatment plan/rationale that is consistent with the explanation of client's distress?)
3. How do you convey a sense of confidence and belief in your treatment approach?

Working Alliance

1. How do you establish goal consensus in the first session?
2. How do you help a client who has no clear goals in therapy?
3. How do you explicitly convey warmth, understanding, and acceptance towards your client?

Client Factors

1. How do you tap into your client's strengths, abilities and resources?

2. How do you enlist and work within your client's values, beliefs, and cultural systems?

Therapist Factors

1. How do you regulate *your* anxiety in a difficult interaction with your clients?
2. How do you manage your counter-transference towards your client?
3. How do you utilise self-disclosure?

(Note: For the comprehensive list, see Taxonomy of Deliberate Practice Activities, TDPA.[1])

You will be tempted to work on a handful of things at a given time. Resist this urge. Your efforts will be unfocused and diffused. Employing the 80/20 principle (work on 20% of the issues to reap 80% of the results), take the following four-step process:

1. **Identify** the potential areas to work on that provides you the leverage on improving engagement;
2. **Rate** each of the items on a scale of 0-10, with 10 being the highest score;
3. **Rank the Top Three** areas in order of priority *(Note: The lowest rated item need not be in the top three, since the top three ranked items should be one that has a direct correlation to improving the engagement),* and
4. Funnel the top three items and pick only one main area to work on. "What is **one key aspect** of my first sessions that I can be working on, so as to improve my engagement levels with clients?" This can be challenging. Narrow down to one thing to work on.[3]

Once you have identified, rated and narrowed down to one area, approach someone who intimately knows your work, like a coach/mentor/supervisor, to do the same process with the TDPA. There is likely to be differences. Concur on what the top three areas are, and then come to a consensus on the key aspect to work on. This becomes *your* individualised learning objective[2].

I encourage you to make the identified learning objective highly **visible**. Refrain from relying solely on your memory of what you are working on. Print it out or write it on a card and put it next to your coffee mug. Date it. Let this card remind you of what's vital.

The final thing to remember is that if there's movement and development in your learning journey, your individualised learning objective doesn't stay the same (that's why you should date it). This process of identifying *what* to work on needs to be repeated on a stipulated routine basis. Don't leave it to "next time." Automate this by setting a date in your calendar to re-view your learning objective. A time-frame of a month or so might be helpful for a start.

See also **46. Deliberate Practice, 48. A Coach, 55. Recording Your First Sessions.**

48. A COACH

Take a close look at competitive sports. Behind every professional team or individual, there is a coach.[1] A good coach is the single most important aspect of improving your performance as a psychotherapist, even if it's specifically aimed at enhancing your first sessions. Your coach plays a vital role in helping you identify *What* to work on.

It may seem odd to be using the term "coach" in psychotherapy, as opposed to the traditional terminology of a clinical supervisor.[2] Our field will do well to apply useful aspects of coaching and teaching to the domain of clinical supervision. I frame coaching as more encompassing than clinical supervision. Coaching includes **coaching for performance** and **coaching for development**.[3]

Differences Between Coaching for Performance and Coaching for Development.

Coaching for Performance	Coaching for Development
Micro	Macro
Traditional case-by-case discussion	Establishing an ongoing learning and development plan, and developing generalisable principles
Improving the outcomes for specific cases	Improving therapist's overall effectiveness
Focus is on the client	Focus is on the therapist

Traditional clinical supervision focuses on *coaching for performance*. This is necessary, but not sufficient. Evidence suggests that clinical supervision does not translate to actual improvement of therapists' outcomes.[4] Therapists need help in dealing with challenging cases, and guidance in developing a professional development roadmap. Going further, therapists will need help with extracting and developing principles that they can learn from challenges and mistakes.[5] Thus, coaching for development goes beyond and provides the therapist with ongoing mentorship (guidance), feeding targeted information when needed (teaching), and helping to cull the excess (editor).

The last point of the coach's role as an editor needs further explanation. Probably the most under-appreciated position in the film industry is the film editor. In Greg McKeown's book *Essentialism*, he points out that the two Oscar awards for "Best Picture" and "Best Film Editing" are highly correlated: "Since 1981 not a single film has won Best Picture without at least being nominated for Film Editing. In fact, in about two-thirds of the cases the movie nominated for Film Editing has gone on to win Best Picture."[6] What is the implication for coaching in psychotherapy? Look for guidance on what to *subtract* from, not add onto, your first sessions.

Coach = Professional Development Needs (micro & macro) +
Mentor (guidance) + Teacher + Editor

You want to make sure that your coach isn't wedded to any particular model of therapy. Rather than starting from a theoretical orientation, you want her to be adaptive to your learning needs. That said, you want a coach who has a good handle on learning principles. She must have a roadmap to help learners grow based on their developmental needs, and provide direction.

If you are looking for a coach, here are the three key elements you will want her to be willing to do:

1. Pay attention to your routine outcomes monitoring (ROM) feedback measures;
2. Watch a handful of your first sessions recordings; and
3. Develop a **learning objective** that befits your developmental learning needs.

(Note: These three points are elaborated in the recommended chapters below. I highly recommend that you provide your coach/supervisor these chapters, so that she gets an idea of how you are systematically trying to improve your craft.)

Renowned basketball coach for the UCLA John Wooden, says it well: "You win by becoming a better player of the game at large, not by adapting your technique to every new team you face. Your opponent will always be changing; it's a losing race. But if you master the game, you will have skills and knowledge you need to defeat whoever you are facing."[7]

See also **3.** The 4Ps vs. The 1P, **44.** The Use of Routine Outcome Monitoring, ROM; **46.** Deliberate Practice, **47.** Individualised Learning Objective; **56.** Recording Your First Sessions.

49. FEEDBACK

Feed-Up, Feed-Back, Feed-Forward

Too often, in the field of psychotherapy, relevant feedback about our performance is lacking. Because psychotherapy can be such a private affair, we often lack the context to work collaboratively at improving our craft. Most of the time, instead of seeking feedback from others about our work and the interaction process in therapy, we spend our time talking about cases, and not "analyzing our game."[1] The expert on expertise, K. Anders Ericsson articulated this concern:

Most professionals – such as doctors, nurses, stockbrokers, and accountants – do not receive the constant pressure from performing in front of an audience of paying ticket holders, like actors, musicians, and athletes. The lack of scrutiny and perhaps feedback may be an important difference that explains why many doctors do not spontaneously adopt the best practice methods for treating their patients, and spend a rather modest amount of time engaged in deliberate practice and effortful training to improve and maintain their skills... The *greatest obstacle for deliberate prac-*

tice during work is the lack of immediate objective feedback (emphasis mine).[2]

When chess players engage in solitary examination of past chess games by masters, they are able to compare their own moves to those of the masters, thus receiving immediate and specific feedback on the quality of their moves. Athletes get virtually immediate feedback by the observable outcome itself, feedback from coaches, as well as delayed viewing of video recordings of their games. Such a feedback loop provides rich and contextual information about their performance, which in turn helps to develop actionable steps toward improvement.

Education researchers John Hattie and Helen Timperley offer a useful feedback model to enhance learning. [3] They suggest that in order for feedback to be effective, these three questions must be answered:

Feed-Up: Where am I going? (What are the goals?)

Feed-Back: How am I going? (What progress is being made toward the goal?), and

Feed-Forward: Where to next? (What activities need to be undertaken to make better progress?)

The feedback process occurs right at the start of the deliberate practice framework, that is, the identification of the learning objective (Feed-Up). Second, the role of a coach is crucial to the mix. This is not to say that self-supervision is not possible. In fact, I highly encourage you to do so. But if you are starting out using this type of outcomes-based approach, it makes a lot of sense to have a coach or mentor guide you.[4]

In order to answer the Feed-Back question of "How am I going?" it is vital you record your sessions. By doing so, discussions that follow will be based on actual review and reflection of the process of therapy, as opposed to a reliance on biased recall and heavy theoretical meaning-making. Subsequently, coach and therapist can discuss the Feed-Forward process of identifying learning activities that can help to take steps towards improvement in the specified area of how you run your first sessions.

If psychotherapy continues to be a "closed door" enterprise, which lacks the level of scrutiny and objective feedback for therapists to improve their work, we won't go very far. We need to *deprivatise* the actual practice of psychotherapy. Only then can we push our clinical effectiveness to the next level.

See also **44. The Use of Routine Outcome Monitoring (ROM), 46. Deliberate Practice, 47. Individualised Learning Objectives, 48. A Coach, 51. Performance Feedback vs. Learning Feedback, 55. Recording Your First Sessions.**

50. SUCCESSIVE REFINEMENT

"My experience is what I agree to attend to."
~William James

W hy doesn't clinical experience make us better therapists? After all, doesn't it take time to get good at something? We know from existing evidence that it does take time to get good, but time doesn't get us good. Studies point out that years of clinical experience is not a predictor of performance. [1] In other words, **clinical practice is not deliberate practice.**

Psychotherapy is one of the few professions in which *practice* actually does not mean a rehearsal but the real thing. It is important not to conflate clinical practice with deliberate practice.

While actual clinical practice is necessary, it is not sufficient to develop and refine the skills of the craft. Clinical practice is not practice in a learning sense. It's the cumulative outcome of all our efforts to be helpful. It's the performance of all that effort that we put in, so that we can be helpful to a wide variety of clients.[2]

On the other hand, deliberate practice is aimed at improving skills in a well-defined manner. The returns are often not immediate: it's rarely monetarily rewarding (in the short term), but it's designed to improve the quality of your clinical practice.

Mere repetition of how you conduct your first sessions is not successive refinement. Successive refinement requires us to **undo** non-engaging practices (i.e., Intake Model approach, see Section I) and improve ways that create an impact on engagement (see Section II).

Successive refinement is an iterative process of correction and re-calibration that is guided by your specific learning objective.[3] This is the *How* to improve, once we have identified the *What* to improve, fleshed out by a pinpoint learning goal and specific feedback provided by your coach. This dynamic process helps you monitor the impact of the targeted refinement based on feedback. In psychotherapy, once the therapist and her coach map out a clear and unambiguous path for deliberate practice, they can adopt a broader vision to monitor not only the level of performance (i.e., outcome), but also how the therapist is implementing and refining what he or she is learning. (See the next chapter.)

See also **46. Deliberate Practice, 47. Individualised Learning Objective, 49. Feedback, 48. A Coach, 51. Performance Feedback Versus Learning Feedback.**

51. PERFORMANCE FEEDBACK VERSUS LEARNING FEEDBACK

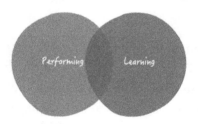

We do not necessarily *learn* from feedback about our performance.[1] At the same time, learning may not necessarily result in improved performance in the short-term. While systematic session-by-session feedback about client progress is vital to ensure success of the therapeutic work, it does not help us learn and improve over time. Let's call this performance feedback (PF). Instead, feedback about how we are *learning* is critical to successful professional development (i.e., getting better outcomes) in the long-run. Let's call this learning feedback (LF).

Learning feedback helps you to perform better. Performance feedback helps you to monitor the impact of your learning.

PF is like the scoreboard in a sports competition. It shows you and your opponent's scores. While the scoreboard is useful, it is difficult to try to learn and perform at the same time. This might explain why in a variety of fields, including psychotherapy, experience does not equate to competence.[2] LF, in contrast, refers to your **learning goals** typically designed in collaboration with your coach/supervisor. For LF to be effective, the coach/supervisor focuses on the immediate objective at hand, without criticising the learner, and breaks the feedback into manageable chunks and enables the clinician to reach beyond their current comfort zone.[3]

Learning typically takes place off-court rather than in the game. What you do off-court matters a lot more than we think.

Once you've enrolled the help of a coach in specifically improving your first sessions, make sure you are receiving not only feedback about your performance, but also how you are applying what you are learning.

See also, **47. Individualised Learning Objectives, 48. A Coach, 55. Recording Your First Sessions, 58. Figure Out Your Circle of Development.**

52. ELICITING CLIENT FEEDBACK

Learning feedback, as described in the previous chapter, can only make sense in the active use of performance feedback. One of the ways to elicit performance feedback is to elicit client feedback using the Session Rating Scale (SRS).[1] This visual analogue scale from 0 to 10 contains four items, asking the client to rate the following:

Relational Bond (How much do you feel heard, understood, and respected?)

Goals/Topics (Did we get to work on and talk about what was important to you today?)

Approach/Method (How does my approach fit with you?)

Overall (In general, how was the session today?)

Alliance is not simply a feeling of connection. That's part of it. Based on the definition of working alliance by Edward Bordin, a therapeutic alliance requires an emotional bond, consensus on the goals of therapy, and a cogent rationale or approach in achieving them.[2] Jerome Frank calls this the consensus of a "believable myth."[3]

Here are three common questions that therapists ask in workshops and consultations about eliciting client feedback:

Q1. Why is measuring engagement level (i.e., the working alliance) important from the first session?

Right from the first session, you want to create an environment of optimal engagement for your client. Our traditional approach of conducting a thorough intake assessment before commencing "therapy" runs the risk of clients prematurely terminating treatment right after the first visit.

When you measure the alliance from the first session, you are communicating three critical things. First, your client's perspective is reality. Second, you are open and receptive to their feedback. Third, it is *your* responsibility, not the client's, to modify, adjust, and recalibrate if the sessions aren't meeting their needs.

How you convey your willingness to change your mind will determine the type of feedback you get.

"Is everything OK today?" will skew the response with a knee-jerk response, "Yeah. All good." Where we point the lens becomes the emphasis. Ask for specific feedback that you are looking out for. Test your suspicions based on the SRS scores and your clinical intuition. For example, "Given the lower scores on the Goals, it's likely I missed something important today. Is that correct?"

Q2. Doesn't the use of measures get in the way of a good rapport?

While it may sound counterintuitive at first, take a moment to process the following: High session rating of engagement by your client is *not* predictive of good outcomes. In contrast, highly effective therapists seem to be able to elicit *low* engagement scores in early sessions.[4] We've also found in our initial *Super-*

shrinks study that, as compared to the average practitioner, highly effective therapists are more likely to report being *surprised by client feedback.* [5] Perhaps supershrinks predispose themselves to be more receptive, and willing to change their minds.[6] High alliance scores in the first session tell us nothing. The client could be truly happy with the session, or she might not feel safe to say to you how you missed the boat. Two entirely different stories.

Here are five things I suggest you can do to set the stage for a culture of feedback in therapy, right from the first session:

I. Provide a Rationale for Eliciting Feedback:

Explain why their feedback is crucial, and what feedback isn't. At this point, sometimes I give two contrasting example between a tailor and a customer feedback survey at a cafe. One seeks to use your opinion to find the best fit for *you*; the other takes your feedback, but does nothing to change your experience. Reinforce the point that "your feedback gives me a chance to make adjustments, changes, or fine-tune the therapy to fit your needs."

II. Prime the Recall:

Consolidate by saying, "today, we talked about __ and we did this exercise __. We came up with some ideas on how to deal with __." You don't have to be teacherly in the way you summarise. You are trying to prime your client's recall, as you ask for his feedback.

III. Pre-Empt the Possible Feedback:

Providing feedback to someone sounds simple, but it's tricky business. Just think about the last time you were asked for feedback. What did you say?

As a therapist, communicate how you will receive the person's point of view. "I will take your feedback seriously, not personally."

"No feedback is too small or insignificant. Even if you think 'Oh, that's a minor issue,' please feel free to share it with me."

VI. How to Ask for Feedback:

For many years, I used to ask this duo-combo question. First, I asked, "What was helpful in today's session?" Then I followed up with, "What wasn't helpful in today's session?" While it was easier for clients to say what was helpful, they often struggled with the second part.

Now, I'm more inclined to ask the following:

*"Based on today's session, what should we do **more** of?"*
and
*"What should we do **less** of?"*

Asking what you should do more of and less of skips the embedded evaluation of "what's helpful and what's not" type of questioning. This allows for a more refined calibration to match the client in future sessions.

V. Encourage Negative Feedback

"You know, giving negative feedback is hard. I want you to know that I'm not looking for high scores. This is not going to be used as a performance evaluation by my boss or anything like that."

If needed, provide your client a concrete example "For instance, we professionals sometimes make the mistake of assuming we know what's best for our clients, which led us to miss the boat on the important topics, and we approached the issue in a less than ideal manner. If that happened today, please score the goals/topics and approach sections (i.e., subscales of the SRS) *lower*."

Be Specific. If you want specific feedback, ask specific questions.

"You know, Kelvin, I got a feeling that I've pushed you too far today, especially when we were attending the issue about your fears. I might have failed to see that this is overwhelming stuff for a first session. Am I mistaken?"

Sometimes it's useful to cite examples of your past client's feedback when appropriate: "You know, I once had a client who told me that I was too careful with her, and she wanted me to just be blatant. Do you feel that way too?" Given how difficult it is for clients to give critical feedback, this approach intentionally slants towards eliciting lower scores. It gives your clients the permission to rate the alliance lower, if it is indeed less than ideal.

Q3. Without using some formal checklist like the SRS, don't we already ask for feedback anyway?

We do, but without an efficient and effective checklist, we often miss what's vital.[7] For example, we might not pick up the nuance that even though a client says she feels good about the session (high Relational Bond score), she feels that there's something else that hasn't been addressed in the first visit (slightly lower Goals score). Using a tool like the SRS sets the stage that you are not going to rush this, and that you value the details what of your clients say. Moreover, when you use formal feedback as part of usual practice, you are less likely to forget asking for feedback. If you took the time to explain the importance of the client's formal feedback in the first session, you would find that in subsequent sessions, it takes less than two minutes to complete this feedback process.

The best way to change the past experience is to redirect your future goals. All feedback should feed-forward. Remember, your client's experience is the key.

See also **49. Feedback, 51. Performance Feedback Versus Learning Feedback, 53. Receiving Client Feedback.**

53. RECEIVING CLIENT FEEDBACK

"One of the most difficult conversations people have is to give and receive negative feedback," says Doug Stone, co-author of the book *Thanks for the Feedback: The Science and Art of Receiving Feedback Well.*[1]

Here's an encounter I had at a newly minted restaurant. It will help illustrate the difficulty of receiving feedback.

"How was your meal sir?"

"Fine, thanks." This couldn't be any further from the truth. Five minutes into the meal, the waitress came back to me. She was wondering why I haven't touched my pasta one bit since she last checked.

"Erm, your meal going ok?"

"Yes, it's fine," I replied, noting the leading question. I smiled, and returned to my conversation with my two friends. The truth was, the pasta was so salty that my mouth was numbed. But I braved on. I was planning to wash it down with a cup of coffee later, and continue our conversation.

The waitress didn't shy away the third time. She stepped in and asked me again, "Sir, is everything ok?" I thought to myself, man, she's persistent. I have to hand it to her. Maybe I should just tell her.

"Actually, since you asked me for the third time, I don't think I'm a fussy eater, but the pasta is so salty that I can't feel my mouth... I can't eat any more of it."

I couldn't have guessed her reply. She came up with a one-liner. Actually, it was just one word. "Oh."

Negotiating the awkward silence, she stepped one foot back and inched away. We couldn't believe what just happened. I'm a hopeful guy. I waited to see if she might return with a replacement, indulge me with a tiramisu cake to sweeten my tooth from the pseudo-anesthesia, or maybe even waive the cost of that half-eaten dish.

None of that happened.

If you ask for feedback, you have to learn to *receive* it.

I once heard a therapist say to a client who was mad at her for making her feel interrogated with a barrage of questions, "Thank you so much for your feedback. It must take so much courage to say what you said." On the surface, it sounds ok to say that. It's polite. It's what we were taught to say. But it isn't helpful.

Let's face it. Is it easy to take negative feedback from your client? Not really. Is it pleasant? Definitely not. Then I think we should be honest and simply say that. "You know, I must admit, this is hard to take in. I'm trying to digest what you are saying... because this is important... What you are saying is that I've been interrogating you, bombing you with question after question. It's hard for me to admit... but you are *right*. Instead of helping you, I've made you feel like a criminal, when you have done nothing wrong... I'm so sorry. I've let you down today. Again, it's tough to hear this, but I really appreciate you telling me this."

When you do get feedback about what didn't go well especially in the first session, treat this as gold. Write down verbatim what your client is saying. Depending on the level of "unhelpfulness," share your reaction. "You know, as hard as it is to hear, I am deeply appreciative of what you are telling me. What I'm hearing you say is that while ___ is bothering you, you'd really want some direction on how to improve _____ instead. Is this correct? I'm sorry I totally missed the boat today. This gives me a chance to rectify and adjust what I'm doing in the subsequent sessions. Please keep this feedback coming." Once again, all feedback must feed-forward.

If you receive high alliance ratings in the first visit, say, "Thanks for your perspective. Tell me, what stands out from today? What's one thing you'd remember most from today's session?" Note down what's most memorable to your client. It's going to inform you on what sticks for that person.

If you receive high alliance ratings in the first session, and it doesn't match with your experience of the session, call it out. Reflect that back to your client, and have a dialogue about it. Do your best to think out loud.

You might be thinking that there's a lot of things to say to receive feedback! There are. It takes about three to five minutes. Without setting the stage, clients won't get how valuable their feedback is. Once you lay the foundations from the first session, on most occasions, the time to elicit feedback at subsequent sessions diminishes significantly.

Clinical supervisors can also benefit from digging deep into learning about how to elicit and receive feedback. It's easy to take for granted the collegial bond, and expect supervisees to vocalise their concerns about the supervisory process when the need arises. I would argue that, *because* of the relationship, it can be even harder to give critical feedback in a supervisory context than in therapy.

Learn to receive feedback as a gift. Zen buddhist monk Thich Nhat Hanh said, "To love without knowing how to love wounds the person we love." To elicit feedback without receiving it well wounds the giver of the feedback.

See also, **49. Feedback, 52. Eliciting Client Feedback.**

54. NOW, LET'S PLAY WITH FEEDBACK

"You're only as young as the last time you changed your mind."
~ Timothy Leary

Once we marry our clinical intuition and the use of outcome-informed data, we can take a step further.

Here's how. I call this the Rate-Predict exercise:

1. **Rate:** At the end of the first session, using an alliance measure (e.g., Session Rating Scale, SRS), ask your client to RATE how they feel about the level of engagement in the session;
2. **Predict:** Before you see your client's score, PREDICT what they would score. It is crucial that you write down scores for each of the sub-scales (for SRS, level of emotional connection, goals, approach/method, overall), and
3. **Evaluate:** Compare and contrast the scores. See what surprised you. Form your feedback questions from there.

There are merits to be in a space of uncertainty. One study found that the more effective therapists are plagued with "professional self-doubt," that is, questioning one's self-efficacy as a therapist.[1] What's more, top performers are more likely to report being surprised by a client's feedback than their counterparts.[2] This does seem to suggest the following:

Highly effective therapists are more willing to be corrected. They have a sense of openness to receive and consider a client's viewpoints, even if it may be contradictory to the therapist's existing expectations.

Janet Metcalfe and colleagues suggest that individuals are more likely to correct errors made with initial high confidence than those made with low confidence, so long as the *corrective feedback* is given. Although it may seem intuitive that deeply held beliefs are more entrenched and are the hardest to change, experimental studies have indicated that individuals are more likely to over-write their responses and correct their beliefs, and are more likely to retain the correct answer compared to knowing the right answer at the outset.[3]

In other words, the Rate-Predict Exercise is set up to intentionally create a context for *seeking the counterfactual*, or **hypercorrection**, not hyper-confirmation.

When we experience hypercorrection, we learn more deeply, as it enhances the memory encoding system. We do not learn when we keep seeking to confirm what we already know.

The late Eugene Gendlin, a pioneer of the focusing approach in therapy, said some years ago before he passed away, when he's asking questions in therapy, he was no longer seeking to be confirmed like he used to. Rather, he's now intentionally seeking to be *disconfirmed* by his client. When we are willing to be wrong, our ears open up.

Try this out. With little trade-off, there's a lot to gain from this simple exercise.

See also **52. Eliciting Client Feedback, 53. Receiving Client Feedback, 45. Why Use Formal Feedback.**

55. RECORDING YOUR FIRST SESSIONS

Would you prefer someone to describe to you in detail about a beautiful song that they heard, or for you to listen to it yourself?

When we talk about a session instead of listening to how it actually went, we recreate it in our heads. We fill in a big gap of reality with our imagination. We create interpretations in the absence of the subject at hand.

Once I was evangelising about the benefits of recording sessions to a group of clinicians, and an experienced therapist said to me, "Yes, it is a brilliant idea. I used to do that as a post-grad student. It's helpful for students... Not so much for me now."

Another said to me, "I cannot stand hearing my own voice in the recordings."

Now imagine this: You are a coach of a tennis player. He comes to you and says that he doesn't want to analyse his videos of the games because he gets uncomfortable looking at himself on-screen. Would you accept that?

Who has a problem with recording the sessions? Mostly, it isn't our clients. It's us. A recent study by a team of researchers found that a majority of clients have no objections to audio/video recording of the sessions, and close to three-quarters of them are willing to consider this. Less than a third of them express discomfort about it.[1]

The value of recording your sessions—especially the first sessions—is priceless. This is why in this chapter, I will be elaborating on how to set this up for you and your clients.

Bring in the audio/video recordings of the session to supervision. It is valuable to examine the start of a session. How we start a session has a ripple effect on how the rest of the hour unfolds. Thereafter, pick the first 15-minute segment for your supervisor/coach to review (see the next two chapters on *Why* and *How* to score the first sessions). This is not only helpful in clinical supervision, but also useful in self-supervision. This clip could be one of the following:

1. A thin slice of the representation of the quality of the engagement;
2. A difficult interaction/alliance rupture moment; or
3. Randomly pick somewhere in the middle of the session. You'd be surprised.

Make recording your sessions as a default practice rather than an exception. This in turn reduces the cognitive load off your mind, given that it's on most of the time, thus fading into the background.[2]

When seeking consent from your clients, provide a social norm of your practice (e.g., "I do this with 90% of my sessions.") and provide a sound rationale on the purpose of recording (e.g., "I record my sessions so that I get to ensure the highest service delivery and experience in therapy... I would review them, when needed, and I might get the help of a supervisor to offer a different perspective."). Clients are more likely to agree when you provide sound reasons.

The rate of compliance to be audio/video recorded is dependent more on the therapist than the client. Clearly, when your client is not comfortable with this idea, do not proceed with the recording. Let them know that their preferences are the priority.

Let's take a step back and consolidate. If you follow the guidelines of this chapter and the earlier chapters in Section III, you would have two important pieces of feedback information: the routine outcome monitoring (ROM) measures, and audio/video recordings of your sessions.

The use of ROM and sessions recordings bring a marriage between the macro and the micro.

When ROM is employed without the use of recordings, you will lack the specificity of what to work on in your learning endeavor. When recordings are used without the context of ROM, you risk walking blind. You wouldn't know if what you've identified as issues are indeed concerns from your client's perspective (i.e., working alliance measures), and you wouldn't know if what you chose to work on has any impact on benefiting clients.

See also **8. Judge Your Assessment, 44. The Use of Routine Outcome Monitoring (ROM), 56. Why Do We Score a First Session? 57. How Do We Score a First Session?**

56. WHY DO WE NEED TO SCORE YOUR FIRST SESSIONS?

Measure the level of impact in your first session to improve on specific segments.

Once you have picked a routine outcome monitoring (ROM) tool to measure your client outcomes and engagement levels, and you have recorded a handful of your first visits, you'd need to find a way to "score" your first sessions.

At its simplest form, like any good story, the first session consists of three parts: A beginning, middle, and an end. [1]

Act I—————————————> Act II ——————————————> Act III
"The Setup"   "The Confrontation"   "The Resolution"

In her book *Resonance*, Nancy Duarte describes Act I as the set-up, Act II as the confrontation/conflict, and Act III as the resolution. Duarte notes that at the end of a dynamic experience, one should end the performance on a higher plane than it began.[2] In psychotherapy, we develop a sense of hope and agency, a new way of seeing our client's situation that is workable in forthcoming sessions, learn something new about herself, and/or soothe some of her predominant symptoms.

From a fundamentalistic Intake Model, the entire first session consists of Act I, eliciting a thorough clinical assessment to set up for the "real" therapy to begin later.

ACT I	ACT II	ACT III
A	A	A
B	B	B
C	C	C
D	D	D
E	E	E

A non-dynamic sequence of an Intake Model that focuses on clinical assessment and does not move beyond "The Setup."

Even in a moderate attempt at the Intake Model, we move from Act I into Act II, stopping short of synthesising the first sessions in the resolution phase of Act III. In this instance, there is little or no signs of a tangible bridge towards the next session.

ACT I	ACT II	ACT III
A	A	A
B	B	B
C	C	C
D	D	D
E	E	E

A sequence that moves from "The Setup" and confronts the challenges, but does not come to a resolution.

ACT I	ACT II	ACT III
A	A	A
B	B	B
C	C	C
D	D	D
E	E	E

A sequence that gets lost in the details of the difficulties and problems.

An impactful session moves through the threes Acts. An Engagement Model not only sees the need for a structure to guide the process of a first session, it appreciates what Joseph Campbell calls the Hero's Journey.[2] At its essential form, the protagonist begins his journey from an Ordinary World (Act I), and he is called to an adventure. He then enters into a Special World (Act

II), committing, experimenting, confronting ordeals and obsta-
cles. Finally, he takes a road back into the Ordinary World (Act
III), and is transformed by the experience.

ACT I	ACT II	ACT III
A	A	A
B	B	B
C	C	C
D	D	D
E	E	E

*A dynamic sequence that engages the client in a clear direction
without getting lost in the weeds.*

ACT I	ACT II	ACT III
A	A	A
B	B	B
C	C	C
D	D	D
E	E	E

A dynamic sequence that explores specific challenges.

What we want to "score" is the **impact of the engagement**.
Daniel Stern points out that in any performing art, be it theatre,
film, or music, there is a sense of *vitality* that takes shape within a

dynamic performance, a deepening of emotional experience, which leads to new emergent themes.[3] When a performance is stale, there is a lack of movement, progression and direction; meandering or derailing.

Differences between Forms of Lifelessness and Forms of Vitality.

Forms of Lifelessness	Forms of Vitality
Static	Movement
No Clear Direction	Directionality
Flat line	Emotional Dynamics
Boredom	Drama

If you measure a "dead" first session—a session that is going nowhere—it would look something like this:

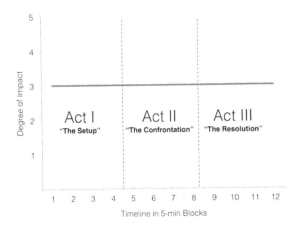

A flat line is an almost guarantee to disengage your client.

Conversely, if you measure the emotional impact of an enlivened and dynamic first session from beginning to end, the graph would look something like this:

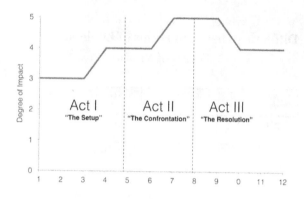

A dynamic first session that engages your client.

Creating forms of vitality in your first sessions is more likely to move and inspire your client.

See also **16. How You Start a First Session? Orient, 17. How You Start a First Session? Reveal Yourself, 18. How You Start a First Session? Regulate "In the Moment" Anxiety, 22. Frame It, 41. How Do You Close a First Session, 55. Recording Your First Sessions, 57. How Do You Score a First Session.**

57. HOW DO WE SCORE A FIRST SESSION?

Segment your first session recordings into 5-min blocks. Analyse and rate the level of impact based on the Impact of Session Grid (ISG).

Before you proceed, you will need some form of recording of your first sessions. For the purposes of this exercise, either video or audio is fine[1]. Once you have a recording, you can put it through the Impact of Session Grid (ISG)[2].

One of the main reasons that it's helpful to use the ISG is that it is fact based rather than based on interpretation. When analysing your sessions, instead of theorising, you want to stay as close as possible to the moment-by-moment reality. What's more, deconstructing the therapy hour into 5-min block helps us think in terms of manageable chunks, and work towards punctuating key moments[3] in the session.

Instructions:

1. **Layout:** Open a spreadsheet. In the top row, mark on each column blocks of five minutes (See image below)

5-min Block Analysis										
Beginning			Middle					End		
0 to 5	5 to 10	10 to 15	15 to 20	20 to 25	25 to 30	30 to 35	35 to 40	40-45	45-50	50-55
3	3	3	3	3	3	4	5	4	3	4

2. **Self-Rating**: At the end of every five minutes, stop the recording and rate that segment from a 0 to 5 Likert-type scale. Start each block with a default of 3 points. (See the following Box for a guide of how you can measure the level of impact in your session).

3. **Coach-Rating**: Once you've scored this, approach a supervisor who is genuinely invested in helping you to get better. Get her to watch your recording, and score the session in the same way. Provide her with the same set of instructions, and start having her rate without seeing your ratings. After your supervisor is done, compare and contrast the spreadsheets.

Impact of Session Grid (ISG) Rating Scale

Ratings:

5. There is a clear **transformative** and a deep engaging experience for the client. Not only has a new emergent theme or a deepening of emotion occurred, the client has shifted from an "ordinary world" into an "extraordinary world" perspective. There is now a clear hope and direction for the future, with an intensity that is not just at an intellectual "head" level, but a dramatic and embodied change for the client, that moves him/her in a desired direction.

4. A **new emergent theme ("new story")** is beginning to unfold, and/or a deepening of a particular theme is occurring. There is a deepening of emotions.. The client sees the rationale and is engaged in where the therapist is facilitating the direction of the therapeutic process.

3. A **neutral** level of interaction. No new emergent theme ("same story") or deepening of emotions. A rating of "3" is normally given when the client is presenting their pre-existing perspective of a situation or a problem.

2. The dynamism of the session is not only static but is beginning to **flatline**. There is a lack of movement or progression in the session.

1. The client is **disengaged** from the process. He or she may be bored or even frustrated that the therapist is not "getting it". The therapist may be trying to go in a different direction and the client is not seeing the rationale for doing so.

Here's a graphical representation of scoring a first session:

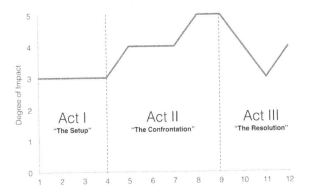

USE OF THE IMPACT OF SESSION GRID (ISG)

Some therapists get overwhelmed that the first session needs to be this dynamic. If you are trying to adhere to a particular method of therapy, you are likely to face difficulty thinking in terms of dynamics and impact. Instead of being invested in solving the problem, well-meaning therapists get unintentionally indoctrinated into a particular solution.

Let's pause for a second: When we watch the first episode of a television series, what do we expect? "Boring" is not in our description. Rather, we expect to be engaged, entranced and "wowed" at the end of the first episode, don't we?

Should we expect anything less in the first session?

See also **55. Recording Your First Sessions, 56. Why Do We Need to Score a First Session.**

58. FIGURE OUT YOUR CIRCLE OF DEVELOPMENT

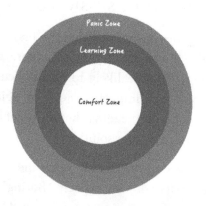

As you saw in Chapter 15, Figure Out Your Client's Circle of Development, you will need to figure out your COD too. The aim of figuring out your comfort zone, learning zone and panic zone is to clarify, magnify, and guide you in your professional development. Having clarity of your COD sharpens your development perspective whenever you begin a first session. In turn, your experience of first sessions will continue to inform you on how to re-define your COD.

Like your clients, your COD is non-static and dynamic. It evolves. So keep yours visible. Draw these three concentric circles, fill them in, date it, and put another date set to review them in the near future (maybe in the next two to three months). Let it be your compass.

Take time to fill in each of the three spaces. Look back over your last week or two of caseloads to make the abstract more concrete.

COMFORT ZONE:

Ask yourself, "What am I used to doing in sessions?" You might even think about, "What did I do well?" "What stands out that I contributed to the development of my client's progress?"

We get comfortable with what we do well. Naturally so. The only problem is, if we fail to take the steps, our comfort zone (CZ) can become our hell zone. What was once helpful can become a problem. Think about your parents. If you were blessed with good enough parents when you were little, imagine if they used the same cuddly warmth and nurturing tendencies with you when you were a teenager. That wouldn't have worked. You would have rebelled with angst. Past attempted solutions can become today's problems.

Here's my current comfort zone (CZ, i.e., things that I do well): Provide clear and playful strategies to clients at the end of each session.

Over the last few years, I found myself drawn to being more playful and improvisational. This wasn't how I used to be. I was constantly plagued with the question, *Am I doing this right?* Then I begin to realise that once I freed myself up to be more playful, I felt more flexible and less certain. This mindset shook things up.

. . .

Other practitioners' CZs that I've come across:

> *"Able to be attentive and follow a clear treatment protocol."*
> *"Exploring a person's strengths and resources."*
> *"Developing clear goals from the beginning."*
> *"Able to attune and empathise with my clients."*

Ask yourself, "What did I do well?" "What stands out that I contributed to the development of my client's progress?" This shall be your comfort zone.

LEARNING ZONE:

The second step is to define your learning zone (LZ). As mentioned previously in the chapter "Figure Out Your Client's Circle of Development," this is related to the zone of proximal development (ZPD).[2] Identifying our learning zone enables us to intentionally stretch the shores of our CZ.

It's important to base your LZ on two critical pieces of information:

I. Your overall outcome data, and
II. Feedback from a coach who knows your work.

By looking at your aggregated outcome data, you can begin to spot any glaring patterns. For example, early in my profession, I was shocked to find out that my outcomes for clients presenting with relational issues were the poorest compared to other presenting concerns, even though I was steeped in systemic perspectives. Your coach's role is to point out what you can't see, and lead you in the right direction.

Here's my current LZ: I would like to learn to help clients face the feelings that they avoid. It's so easy to keep validating and get lost in the interaction with my clients, but miss the opportunity to go deeper and help them with their difficult and painful emotions.

Other common LZs that I've come across:

> *"I would like to learn to improve the way I start my sessions."*
> *"I would like to learn to improve the way I close my first sessions."*
> *"I would like to learn to improve the way I elicit feedback at the close of a session."*

An excellent way to think about developing your LZ statement is to do this sentence completion exercise: "I would like to learn to..." Take it as a given that you will be struggling with this for a while. Give yourself time for this. Avoid non-specific definitions like, "I want to improve my engagement skills." Narrow down to something more concrete and workable.

If your data suggest that many of your clients come only for one session and drop out after that, you may be tempted to state that your LZ is "...to improve my return rates after the first session." I see this more as an *outcome* goal. That is, you want X to influence Y, and "Y" is your outcome goal. In this case, you need to specify X and work on this. Hint: You can revisit the chapters in Section Two: Increase Your Impact to get some ideas.

Once you've taken a stab at identifying your learning zone, approach a mentor/coach/ supervisor, and ask them for their opinion. How would they complete this sentence? A word of caution: Do not ask someone who doesn't know your work. We wouldn't expect a coach to give an athlete any specific advice without knowing how they actually perform in the game.

PANIC ZONE:

Figuring out our current Panic Zone (PZ) is as important as defining our CZ and LZ. Don't skip this step. Once again, I refer to PZ as the tipping point where things get overwhelming and we start to fight, flight, freeze or fall asleep. PZ can also remind you what *not* to do, or what *not* to focus on.

Here's my current Panic Zone (PZ): Trying to improve in more than one area at a time!

One of my biggest issues at this time of writing is that I'm overwhelmed. I'm often tempted to read, learn and work on too many areas at one time! I've got stacks of next in line books, articles, videos, projects, and online courses, all running in parallel. I can feel my mind getting diffused, and I'm frustrated. Instead of trying to do several things in parallel, I found that I'm much better off doing things in *series*. That is, as simple as it sounds, to do one key thing at a time. This helps me to devote my energy and focus deep into one selected project, and only move on to the next thing once the initial project is completed.

I remind myself to keep my eyes on the Taxonomy of Deliberate Practice Activities (TDPA; see chapter Individualised Learning Objectives), which highlights the thing that I'm working on right now. I look at my TDPA, and then I make a plan and put a specific date and time in my schedule to revisit and revise the learning objectives.

Other common Panic Zones that I've come across:

> *"Trying to learn what my supervisor says I should be focusing on, when I do not fully agree."*
> *"I know I should be working on difficult emotions like anger, but I do not feel ready at this point."*
> *"I tend to take critical feedback personally."*

"I just do not have the time and energy for this."

The last statement is worth the elaboration. Be honest with yourself. If this applies to you, it may mean that you've got too much on your plate.

Do not mistake exhaustion for laziness. If you are overworked and your energy is spent on performing at your work, something needs to be done. A system needs to be in place to replenish you. Not just once, but on a routine basis.[3]

The next step we need to do is to build walls. If we do not build pillars of protected time for learning, we will continue to be sucked into the whirlwind of work.

Experiencing deep learning and professional development is inoculative of burnout.

Treat investment in time for deep learning as a form of energy refueling. Just like our drive to the petrol station, it needs to happen routinely.

Keep your circle of development (COD) as a visible dashboard. Pin it on the front of your desk. Put the current date on it and add another future date set to revisit it. Keep your eyes on the ball. Revere your Panic Zone and direct all your energy toward your Learning Zone, and watch it slowly evolve into your comfort zone.

See also, 15. Figure Out Your Client's Circle of Development, 33. Past Attempted Solutions, 44. The Use of Routine Outcome Monitoring (ROM), 47. Individualised Learning Objectives, 48. A Coach.

SUMMARY OF KEY POINTS TO BUILDING A CULTURE OF LEARNING

Here are the key points to building a culture of learning in a first session.

Chapters	Keys to Building a Culture of Learning
44. The Use of Routine Outcome Monitoring (ROM)	ROM = Evaluation + Improvement
45. Why Use Formal Feedback?	Data + Intuition = Better Decisions.
46. Deliberate Practice	Employ the principles of a deliberate practice framework to translate your learning into outcomes.
47. Individualised Learning Objective	Figure out *What* to work on before *How* to get better.
48. Coach	Coach = Professional Development Needs (micro & macro) + Mentor (guidance) + Teacher + Editor
49. Feedback	Feed-Up, Feed-Back, Feed-Forward.
50. Successive Refinement	Develop opportunities for the iterative process of correction and re-calibration.
51. Performance Feedback Versus Learning Feedback	Learning feedback helps you to perform better. Performance feedback helps you to monitor the impact of your learning.
52. Eliciting Client Feedback	How you convey your willingness to change your mind will determine the type of feedback you get.
53. Receiving Client Feedback	If you ask for feedback, you have to learn to *receive* it.
54. Now, Let's Play with Feedback	Enlist the Rate-Predict Exercise. We learn best when we are surprised by our inaccuracies.
55. Recording Your First Sessions	Marry routine outcome monitoring (ROM) with your session recordings to paint a rich picture of your work.
56. Why Do We Need to Score a First Session?	Measure the level of impact in your first session so as to improve on specific segments.
57. How Do We Score a First Session?	Segment your first session recordings into 5-min blocks. Analyse and rate the level of impact based on the Impact of Session Grid (ISG).
58. Figure Out Your Circle of Development	Step out of your comfort zone, and into your learning zone... But know where your panic zone is.

CONCLUSION: ANY OLD MAP WILL DO

"Those are my principles, and if you don't like them... well, I have others." ~ Groucho Marx

A small group of Hungarian troops was camped in the Alps during the First World War. Their commander, a young lieutenant, decided to send a small group of men on a scouting mission. Shortly after they left, snow began to fall steadily for two days. The scouting squad did not return, and the young officer, something of an intellectual and an idealist, suffered a paroxysm of guilt over having sent his men to their deaths. In his torment he questioned not only his decision to send out the scouting mission, but also the war itself and his own role in it.

On the third day, the long-overdue scouting squad returned. There was great joy and relief in the camp, and the young commander questioned his men eagerly. "Where were you?" he asked. "How did you survive? How did you find your way back?" The sergeant who had led the scouts replied, "We were lost in the snow and we had given up hope and resigned ourselves to die. Then one of the men found a map in his pocket. With its help we knew we could find our way back. We made camp, waited for the snow to stop, and then as soon as we could travel we returned here." The young commander asked to see this wonderful map. It was a map not of the Alps but of the Pyrenees![1]

We like to believe that our practices are based on sound theories. More often, theories of psychotherapy are built post-hoc. "The theorists can only build his theories about what the practitioner was doing yesterday. Tomorrow the practitioner will be doing something different because of these theories," says Gregory Bateson. It is after the fact that we develop a theory of our own. It would be naive to believe that when we develop such theories and schools of thought, they would apply to the general population of psychotherapists.

What I hope you took away from this book were key **principles**[2] —not methods—in developing your own ideas on how to run a first session. The field of psychotherapy is awash with hundreds of methods of how to skin a cat. Instead, dig a little deeper and see the first principles operating at the fundamental level. At the end of each of the three Sections, the key tables list this out. For instance, in Chapter 3: The Perils of the Intake Model, the principle is to *Give*, not to *Take*. Another example: In Chapter 18: "What is Your View of the Problem," the principle is to do more "perspective getting" than "perspective taking." Go back to the three tables and refer to them. (See next, *A Gift for You*.)

The principles of this book are based on the Engagement Model of relating to people we meet FOR THE FIRST TIME. It's not a doctrine to follow, but a map. It's not even *the* map, but a guiding compass I hope can break us out of the Intake model, and ignite our first sessions in psychotherapy.

Go play with these ideas, and develop your own principles.

A GIFT FOR YOU

Reading a book is a tremendous opportunity cost and investment of time. I heard someone say "people don't read books anymore." I want to thank you for making it to the end.

This book aims to help you implement these ideas in the way you conduct your first sessions. It's not just meant to be a good read, but it's intended to make good the experience of the first sessions for your clients.

As my gift for you, I want to provide you a set of materials to help you through this process of igniting your first sessions:

- A pocket guide for each of the three sections of the book;
- A Taxonomy of Deliberate Practice Activities (TDPA);
- Circle of Development worksheets;
- A cheat-sheet for using the Outcome Rating Scale and Session Rating Scale;
- A template consent form for asking clients for permission to audio/video record sessions,
- And much more!

Go to darylchow.com/firstkiss to download the resources. Email me if you have questions at info@darylchow.com

IMPLEMENTATION:

Ideas are useful only if we execute them. If you or your agency need help in implementing these ideas in how you conduct first sessions in therapy, drop me an email at the same address above to schedule a consult.

My aim is not to create a mass audience with this book. It's not for everyone. Instead, I want to create a personal connection with you. Let me know what you think of this book. What are your challenges, and what you have achieved from applying these ideas. Let's keep the conversation alive.

GRATITUDE

Anything worth doing requires more than an individual.

I'm deeply grateful to Scott Miller, who has been my mentor and friend for so many years. His unwavering spirit to seek the truth has been contagious in my personal and professional life. Thank you, Scott, for pulling me out of my shell, and galvanising me into the world of research and training. And for having me as co-teacher and a collaborator in all the interesting projects we have worked on. We have only just begun.

Bruce Wampold moved and inspired me through the years in a profound and instrumental way in his writings. Like Scott, through the years in our communication and kind support, you gave me the courage to move along, even though I didn't quite have the confidence.

I want to thank Birgit Villa, Jeanice Cheong, Rashidah Sulaiman and Bob Beckwith for going through the manuscript at the early stages of its conception. Sharon Lu has been a big help for bouncing off my ideas and helping me articulate some of my thoughts, while we were also working through the Difficult

Conversations in Therapy (DCT) clinical trial in the last three years. Big thanks to Ben Mullings and Kaye Frankcom for providing valuable feedback before I let this book go.

Big appreciation to my editor Shawn Mihalik for the successive refinement, and for bearing with me through the delays as I plowed through the many drafts that I was working on—while you were in the midst of moving to another state! Thanks to Emma J. Hardy for the cover design. Simplicity is so hard to achieve. I'm so grateful to my dear friend, Jeremiah Ang for the photography.

Thank you to all whom I've mentored/supervised. You allowed me to be playful with my ideas, and your feedback helped me to feed-forward what was useful, and what needed to be weeded out.

I'm indebted to Juliana Toh, my long-time supervisor and mentor, who is spirited in so many ways. Above all, she has taught me the rudiments of what it means to be life-giving.

Jeff Zeig laid an essential seed in the ideas in Section II. In 2010, I was first introduced to the idea of creating "impact" during his hypnosis workshops. I'm grateful to Jeff for taking the extra time to have dinner and to share with me the ideas that you were working on for your documentary.

To my dear wife and two daughters. I have been Mr. Grouch through the process of writing this book. And it has been a long time. Please forgive me. May I learn to write without causing pain to the family; may I learn to see you each morning, as if for the first time, for our first kiss.

NOTES

I chose not to write a reference list in APA style, as I wanted readers who are intrigued by any of the topics I wrote about in this book, to easily dive deeper into the references that inspired me in each chapter. I also provided some commentaries and recommendations here, so as not to distract you from the central thesis of this book.

Introduction

1. I was first introduced to doing this in 2004 when a friend of mine shared this book with me.

Duncan, B. L., Miller, S. D., & Sparks, J. A. (2004). *The heroic client: A revolutionary way to improve effectiveness through client-directed, outcome-informed therapy (rev. ed.).* San Francisco, California: Jossey-Bass Inc.

For a good pioneering example of collecting client outcomes in private practice, see the late Paul Clement's work below. He has been publishing his outcomes for the past 40 years. Clement serves as a true inspiration to all of us.

Clement, P. P. A. (2013). Practice-Based Evidence: 45 Years of Psychotherapy's Effectiveness in a Private Practice. *American Journal of Psychotherapy, 67*(1), 23-46.

Clement, P. W. (2008). Outcomes from 40 years of psychotherapy in a private practice. *American Journal of Psychotherapy, 62*(3), 215-239.

Clement, P. W. (1994). Quantitative evaluation of 26 years of private practice. *Professional Psychology: Research and Practice, 25*(2), 173-176. doi:http://dx.doi.org/10.1037/0735-7028.25.2.173

2. Chow, D. L., & Lu, S. (2015). *The use of routine outcome monitoring in an asian outpatient psychiatric setting.* Paper presented at the World Federal of Mental Health., Singapore.

3. Mander, H. (2014). The impact of additional initial face-to-face sessions on engagement within an Improving Access to Psychological Therapies service. *The Cognitive Behaviour Therapist, 7*, 1-8. doi:10.1017/S1754470X13000007

4. Baekeland, F., & Lundwall, L. (1975). Dropping out of treatment: A critical review. *Psychological Bulletin, 82*(5), 738-783.

5. Barrett, M. S., Chua, W.-J., Crits-Christoph, P., Gibbons, M. B., & Thompson, D. O. N. (2008). Early withdrawal from mental health treatment: Implications for psychotherapy practice. *Psychotherapy: Theory, Research, Practice, Training, 45*(2), 247-267.

6. Interview with James Altucher #184: http://traffic.libsyn.com/altucher/JAS-184-RobertCialdini-vo1-FREE.mp3

7. The quote from David Foster Wallace was cited in

Kleon, A. (2014). *Show your work: 10 Ways to share your creativity and get discovered.* United States of America: Workman Publishing Co, Inc.

SECTION I: BREAKING THE SACRED RULES

1. Intake Second (Not First)

1. A word of caution. I am aware that the use of the word *model* to a bunch psychotherapists is dangerous. I do not mean a school of therapy. All I am suggesting is a different framework to approach and organise our ways of thinking.

For a thorough review of the operational definition of client engagement, check out

Holdsworth, E., Bowen, E., Brown, S., & Howat, D. (2014). Client engagement in psychotherapeutic treatment and associations with client characteristics, therapist characteristics, and treatment factors. *Clinical Psychology Review, 34*(5), 428-450. doi:http://dx.doi.org/10.1016/j.cpr.2014.06.004

2. This echoes Carl Rogers unforgettable words: "In my early professional years I was asking the question: How can I treat, or cure, or change this person? Now I would phrase the question in this way: How can I provide a relationship which this person may use for his own personal growth?" (p.32)

Rogers, C. (1961). *On Becoming a Person*. New York: Houghton Mifflin Company.

3. Rogers, C. R. (1980). *A way of being*. New York: Houghton Mifflin Company.

4. Nielsen, S. L., Okiishi, J., Nielsen, D. L., Hawkins, E. J., Harmon, C. S., Pedersen, T., . . . Jackson, A. P. (2009). Termination, Appointment Use, and Outcome Patterns Associated With Intake Therapist Discontinuity. *Professional Psychology Research & Practice June, 40*(3), 272-278.

2. The Perils of an Intake Model

1. Articles that cite the average number of sessions attended by clients:

Baldwin, S. A., Berkeljon, A., Atkins, D. C., Olsen, J. A., & Nielsen, S. L. (2009). Rates of Change in Naturalistic Psychotherapy: Contrasting Dose-Effect and Good-Enough Level Models of Change. *Journal of Consulting & Clinical Psychology, 77*(2), 203-211. doi:10.1037/a0015235

Hansen, N. B., Lambert, M. J., & Forman, E. M. (2002). The psychotherapy dose-response effect and its implications for treatment delivery services. *Clinical Psychology: Science and Practice, 9*(3), 329-343. doi:http://dx.doi.org/10.1093/clipsy/9.3.329

2. I first learned about this from a workshop by Michael Yapko. Since then, when I examined the data of agencies I consult with who are on the cutting edge of measuring their own outcomes, I noticed this trend as well. And often, managers do not pick this up, as it is often not included in the analysis of effectiveness, because for those clients who come for only one session, they do not have a pre-post measure comparison.

3. See Nassim Taleb's preliminary draft of Skin in the Game: http://www.fooledbyrandomness.com/minority.pdf This book has since been released.

3. The 4P's versus the 1P

1. I highly recommend reading Greg Mckeown's book in its entirety.

Mckeown, G. (2014). *Essentialism: The disciplined pursuit of less.* Great Britain: Random House Group Company.

2. See Adam Morgan and Mark Baden's 2015 book, A Beautiful Constraint.

Morgan, A., & Barden, M. (2015). *A beautiful constraint: How to transform your limitations into advantages and why it's everyone's business.* New Jersey: Wiley.

3. See The Art of Manliness blogpost on the law of sacrifice: http://www.artofmanliness.com/2011/07/14/blacksmithing-primer

4. Avoid TBU ("True But Useless") Information

1. Heath, C., & Heath, D. (2011). *Switch: How to change things when change is hard.* New York: Random House Inc.

5. Make Them First

1. Robert Cialdini's. work on persuasion is highly recommended. See his two books:

Cialdini, R. B. (2016). *Pre-suasion: A revolutionary way to influence and persuade.* New York: Simon & Schuster.

Cialdini, R. B. (1993). *Influence: The Psychology of Persuasion.* New York: William Morrow and Company, Inc.

6. Remove the Gatekeeper...

1. Wise, M. J., & Rinn, R. C. (1983). Premature client termination from psychotherapy as a function of continuity of care. *Journal of Psychiatric Treatment and Evaluation, 5,* 63–65.

2. Nielsen, S. L., Okiishi, J., Nielsen, D. L., Hawkins, E. J., Harmon, C. S., Pedersen, T., . . . Jackson, A. P. (2009). Termination, Appointment Use, and Outcome Patterns Associated With Intake Therapist Discontinuity. *Professional Psychology Research & Practice June,* 40(3), 272-278.

3. Baldwin, Wampold and Imel (2007) found that the 97% of the variance between therapists was explained by the therapists' ability in alliance formation. This high percentage of the variance explained is not often heard of in social sciences. It's important to note that client's ability in alliance formation, the interaction

between client and therapist in alliance ratings, and early symptom change, did not predict outcomes. In other words, some therapists are simply more effective with a wide range of clients!

Baldwin, S. A., Wampold, B. E., & Imel, Z. E. (2007). Untangling the Alliance-Outcome Correlation: Exploring the Relative Importance of Therapist and Patient Variability in the Alliance. *Journal of Consulting & Clinical Psychology, 75*(6), 842-852. doi:10.1037/0022-006X.75.6.842

7. ...If Not, Be the Gate Opener of Client Preferences

1. Swift, J. K., & Greenberg, R. P. (2015). *Premature termination in psychotherapy: Strategies for engaging clients and improving outcomes.* Washington, DC: American Psychological Association.

2. The two meta-analyses:

Swift, J. K., Callahan, J. L., & Vollmer, B. M. (2011). Preferences. In J. C. Norcross (Ed.), *Psychotherapy relationships that work* (2nd ed., pp. 301–315). New York, NY: Oxford University Press. doi:10.1093/acprof:oso/9780199737208.003.0015

Swift, J. K., Callahan, J. L., Ivanovic, M., & Kominiak, N. (2013). Further examination of the psychotherapy preference effect: A meta-regression analysis. *Journal of Psychotherapy Integration, 23,* 134–145. doi:10.1037/a0031423

3. The rating and ranking approach was borrowed from this article:

Crits-Christoph, P., Gallop, R., Diehl, C. K., Yin, S., & Gibbons, M. B. (2016). Methods for Incorporating Patient Preferences for Treatments of Depression in Community Mental Health Settings. *Adm Policy Ment Health.* doi:10.1007/s10488-016-0746-1

8. Judge Your Assessment

1. Needless to say, please seek your clients' permission to do so,

while keeping to the ethical practice of your state/country/professional body.

9. Do the Prep

1. There is a book on the topic of mental preparation called Psyched Up, by Daniel McGinn.

McGinn, D. (2017). *Psyched up: How the science of mental preparation can help you succeed.* New York: Penguin Random House.

10. Listen in Order to Question, or Question in Order to Listen?

1. Beckwith, H., & Beckwith, C. (2007). *You, Inc.: The art of selling yourself.* New York: Hachette Book Group.

2. I highly recommend you read these three-part series of articles by psychiatrist and family therapist, Karl Tomm:

Tomm, K. (1987). Interventive interviewing: I. Strategizing as a fourth guideline for the therapist. *Family Process, 26*(1), 3-13.

Tomm, K. (1987). Interventive interviewing: II. Reflexive questioning as a means to enable self-healing. *Family Process, 26*(2), 167-183.

Tomm, K. (1988). Interventive interviewing: III. Intending to ask lineal, circular, strategic, or reflexive questions? *Family Process, 27*(1), 1-15.

11. Gifting: Give a Gift

This was shared with me by Jeff Zeig. For more on Milton Erickson, check out this documentary, The Wizard in the Dessert https://catalog.erickson-foundation.org/category/biographical-video

I highly recommend George Burns' book 101 Healing Stories. This is not just for the stories, but Burns provides a good outline on how to use metaphors and create your own stories (PRO, problem resource, outcome) approach in weaving a useful narrative for your client.

Burns, G. (2001). *101 Healing stories: Using metaphors in therapy.* New York: John Wiley & Sons.

3. I first learned about this story from Derek Sivers blog: https://sivers.org/horses

4. See http://literarydevices.net/aphorism/

12. Secularise Spirituality

1. Scott Miller and Mark Hubble provided some powerful examples in their article in Psychotherapy Networker. A thought provoking read.

Miller, S. D., & Hubble, M. (2017). How psychotherapy has lost its magick. *Psychotherapy Networker, March/April.*

13. Assessing Risk From Both Sides

1. Large et al. (2016) analysed over 40 years of data on suicide risk assessment. Although there is an association between high-risk groups and completed suicide, "about half of all suicides are likely to occur in lower-risk groups....(and) 95% of high-risk patients will not suicide."

Large, M., Kaneson, M., Myles, N., Myles, H., Gunaratne, P., & Ryan, C. (2016). Meta-Analysis of Longitudinal Cohort Studies of Suicide Risk Assessment among Psychiatric Patients: Heterogeneity in Results and Lack of Improvement over Time. *PLoS ONE, 11*(6), e0156322. doi:10.1371/journal.pone.0156322

2. Flemons, D., & Granlnik, L. M. (2013). *Relational suicide assessment: Risks, resources, and possibilities for safety.* New York: W. W. Norton & Company.

3. The same meta-analysis by Large et al. (2016) found no

evidence that our suicide risk assessment strategies have improved over time.

However, more innovative and novel approach to assessment suicide risk holds promising possibilities for the way forward. Consider Matthew Nock and his team of researchers (2010) suggests the possibility of using behavioral markers to predict suicidal behavior. Specifically, the use of an implicit association test (IAT) aimed at tapping into people's implicit cognitions of themes between death/suicide with self. Compared to the usual known predictors (e.g., depression, past suicide-attempts) obtained from an assessment as determined from both patients' and clinicians' prediction, they were able to increase the odds of accurate prediction with IAT by 6-fold. I have not held of anything quite this dramatic as yet.

For more about implicit associations, check out the following book:

Banaji, M. R., & Greenwald, A. G. (2013). *Blindspots: Hidden biases of good people*. New York: Random House Publishing.

14. Get Over the Sacred Cow of "Adhering to the Model"

1. Webb, C. A., DeRubeis, R. J., & Barber, J. P. (2010). Therapist adherence/competence and treatment outcome: A meta-analytic review. *Journal of Consulting and Clinical Psychology, 78*(2), 200-211. doi:http://dx.doi.org/10.1037/a0018912 (page 207)

2. Owen, J., & Hilsenroth, M. J. (2014). Treatment Adherence: The Importance of Therapist Flexibility in Relation to Therapy Outcomes. *Journal of Counseling Psychology, 61*(2), 280-288.

3. Hattie, J., & Yates, G. C. (2014). *Visible learning and the science of how we learn*. New York: Routledge.

4. Interview with Paul McCartney on NPR, All Songs Considered:

http://www.npr.org/sections/allsongs/2016/06/10/481256944/all-songs-1-a-conversation-with-paul-mccartney Here's the full quote on what Paul says to the students in a songwriting class in Liverpool Institute High School for Boys: "I don't know how to do this. You would think I do, but it's not one of these things you ever know how to do. You know I can say to you: Select the key. We will now select a rhythm. Now make a melody. Now think of some great words,' That's not really the answer."

(An aside: I actually applied to the Liverpool Institute for Performing Arts (LIPA) when I was 18 years old. I went in with my guitar, and flopped at all the theories they threw at me. Then I was told I could go to the songwriting or sound engineering course instead. Maybe if I went to LIPA, I could defer my compulsory National Service in the army. I didn't tell my parents. And I wasn't really serious about moving to Liverpool anyway.)

SECTION II: INCREASING YOUR IMPACT

15. Figure Out Your Client's Circle of Development

1. Vygotsky, L. S. (1978). *Mind in society: The development of higher psychological processes.* Cambridge, MA: Harvard University Press.

16. How Do You Start a First Session? Orient.

1. An aside: In some cultures, asking a person, "Have you eaten?" sounds odd. Why would you care if someone had their lunch or not? In Asian cultures, this is more like a greeting. It is like saying, "How are you?" in a Western context.

17. How Do You Start a First Session? Reveal Yourself

1. Ori Brafman and Rom Brafman (2010) point out five key factors that help accelerate connection between two people: Vulnerability, proximity, resonance, similarity, and a safe place. For more details, read their highly engaging book, *Click*.

Brafman, O., & Brafman, R. (2010) *Click: The forces behind how we fully engage with people, work, and everything we do*. New York: Crown Business.

2. Youngme Moon (2000) devised an interesting social experiment on how consumers self-disclose personal information to a computer. She discovered that participants were more likely to share vulnerable, personal information, when the computer revealed itself. For example, instead of the computer asking the question, "What have you done in your life that you feel most guilty about?" the computer "opened up" first: "This computer is usually used on a daily basis by many different users. Sometimes, however, many days go by without anyone using it at all. This usually happens over the holidays. So this computer ends up just sitting here, for days and days, with absolutely nothing to do," and then the question is asked. The participants knew that this was a computer, not a person. And they rated the computer that they've interacted with as more likeable, friendly, kind, and helpful!

Moon, Y. (2000). Intimate Exchanges: Using Computers to Elicit Self-Disclosure from Consumers. *Journal of Consumer Research, 26*(4), 323-339.

3. Ta, V. P., Babcock, M. J., & Ickes, W. (2016). Developing Latent Semantic Similarity in Initial, Unstructured Interactions: The Words May Be All You Need. *Journal of Language and Social Psychology*. doi:10.1177/0261927x16638386

4. This is an interview Tami Simon had with Parker Palmer, featured in Sounds True production (2015). An Undivided life: Seeking Wholeness in Ourselves, Our Work and Our World.

18. How Do You Start a First Session? Regulate "In-the-Moment" Anxiety

1. I highly recommend you to check out Jon Frederickson's 2013

book, Co-Creating Change. To my knowledge, even though this was written in a short-term psychodynamic language, this is the only book I've seen that addresses regulating anxiety within the process of therapy. It offers specific signals to look out on how a client is managing anxiety, and moment-by-moment interaction on what to do if a client employs defenses or cognitive disruptions.

Frederickson, J. (2013). *Co-creating change: Effective dynamic techniques.* Kansas City, MO: Seven Leaves Press.

19. "What is Your View of the Problem?"

1. "The weakness of perspective taking is obvious..." from the Mindwise book, p. 168.

Epley, N. (2014). *Mindwise: How we understand what others think, believe, feel, and want.* Great Britain: Penguin Group.

2. Krznaric, R. (2014). *Empathy: Why it matters, and how to get it.* Great Britain: Random House Group.

20. The Goal May be to Figure Out the Goal

1. See Derek Sivers blogpost: https://sivers.org/goals

21. Define the Lead Story

1. I first heard this story in a remarkable book by Chip and Dan Heath, Made To Stick (2007, pp. 75-76). Here's the link to that original story: nwscholasticpress.org/2013/06/18/the-best-journalism-teacher-i-ever-had/

Heath, C., & Heath, D. (2007). *Made to stick: Why some ideas survive and others die.* New York: Random House Inc.

22. Frame It

1. *"I wouldn't let her have these problems,"* see location 158 of 2863 of ebook.

Yapko, M. (2016). *The Discriminating therapist: Asking "how" questions, making distinctions, and finding direction in therapy*. Fallbrook, CA, USA: Yapko Publications.

2. While framing a person's problems using a psychiatric label might be helpful for some, this form of diagnostic laden languaging might be disempowering for others, and does not capture the individual's social context and personal lived experience.

3. Ecker, B., Ticic, R., & Hulley, L. (2012). *Unlocking the emotional brain: Eliminating symptoms at their roots using memory reconsolidation*. New York: Routledge.

24. Follow the Pain

1. "Developing a pain compass," see pp. 144-145 in Greenberg, L., & Watson, J. C. (2006). *Emotion-focused therapy for depression*. Washington, DC: APA.

2. *"Pitch a tent. Set up camp right there."* as cited on page 51 of Ecker, B., Ticic, R., & Hulley, L. (2012).

Unlocking the emotional brain: Eliminating symptoms at their roots using memory reconsolidation. New York: Routledge.

25. Follow the Spark

1. Gassmann, D., & Grawe, K. (2006). General Change Mechanisms: The Relation Between Problem Activation and Resource Activation in Successful and Unsuccessful Therapeutic Interactions. *Clinical Psychology & Psychotherapy, 13*(1), 1-11. doi:http://dx.doi.org/10.1002/cpp.442

2. Cal Fussman was interviewed a second time on the Tim Ferriss Show. see: https://tim.blog/2016/08/31/cal-fussman-the-master-storyteller-returns/. The segment about best strategies to get to the heart of an interview is at 2:04:12 segment.

26. Raising Expectations

1. Murkoff, H., & Mazel, S. (2016). *What to expect when you are expecting* (5th ed.). New York: Workman Publishing.

2. Simon, C. (2016). *Impossible to ignore: Creating memorable content to influence decisions*. New York: McGraw-Hill, Education.

27. The Role of The Therapist

1. Fancher, R. T. (1995). *Cultures of healing: Correcting the image of American mental health care*. New York, W.H. Freeman.

28. The Role of Client

1. Burns, D. D., & Spangler, D. L. (2000). Does psychotherapy homework lead to improvements in depression in cognitive-behavioral therapy or does improvement lead to increased home-work compliance? *Journal of Consulting and Clinical Psychology, 68*(1), 46-56. doi:http://dx.doi.org/10.1037/0022-006X.68.1.46

29. What to Expect

1. Devilly, G. J., & Borkovec, T. D. (2000). Psychometric properties of the credibility/expectancy questionnaire. *Journal of Behavior Therapy and Experimental Psychiatry, 31*(2), 73-86. doi:10.1016/S0005-7916(00)00012-4

2. Constantino, M. J. (2012). Believing is seeing: An evolving research program on patients' psychotherapy expectations. *Psychotherapy Research, 22*(2), 127-138. doi:http://dx.doi.org/10.1080/10503307.2012.663512

3. Given the evidence that the closer the gap between sessions impacts the speed of recovery, in most circumstances, I would suggest a weekly session for the initial stages of therapy, so as to optimise gains early on, and then spread out the sessions later on. See Erekson, D. M., Lambert, M., & Eggett, D. L. (2015). The relationship between session frequency and

psychotherapy outcome in a naturalistic setting. *Journal of Consulting & Clinical Psychology, 83*(6), 1097-1107. doi:http://dx.-doi.org/10.1037/a0039774

30. Sweet Anticipation

1. See p.100 of Simon, C. (2016). *Impossible to ignore: Creating memorable content to influence decisions.* New York: McGraw-Hill, Education.

2. The original quote is attributed to German psychiatrist Frieda Fromm-Reichmann "The patient does not need an interpretation, but a new experience."

31. Exercising Restraint: Tag It

1. The researchers identified four factors that influence choice overload:

- The difficulty of the decision task;
- The complexity of the choice set;
- When preferences are unclear, and
- When the aim is to make a quick easy choice.

Chernev, A., Böckenholt, U., & Goodman, J. (2015). Choice overload: A conceptual review and meta-analysis. *Journal of Consumer Psychology, 25*(2), 333-358. doi: http://dx.doi.org/10.1016/j.jcps.2014.08.002

2. Koriat, A., & Bjork, R. A. (2006). Illusions of competence during study can be remedied by manipulations that enhance learners' sensitivity to retrieval conditions at test. *Memory & Cognition, 34*(5), 959-972. doi:10.1037/0278-7393.31.2.187

3. Anderson, T., Lunnen, K. M., & Ogles, B. M. (2010). Putting models and techniques in context. In B. L. Duncan, S. D. Miller, B. E. Wampold, & M. A. Hubble (Eds.), *The heart and soul of*

change: Delivering what works in therapy (2nd ed., pp. 143-166). Washington, DC: American Psychological Association.

Frank, J. D., & Frank, J. B. (1993). *Persuasion and healing: A comparative study of psychotherapy* (3rd ed.). Baltimore: Johns Hopkins University Press.

32. Ask "Who"

1. Incidentally, 'Poppy' is referred to Grandfather in Australia. But back in my home country in Singapore, my mother's grandkids calls her that! It's a short-form for 'Po Po', which is a derivative based in Mandarin for Grandmother.

2. See Fred Rogers accepting the Lifetime Achievement Award at the 24th Annual Daytime Emmy Awards: youtube.com/watch?v=Upm9LnuCBUM

33. Past Attempted Solutions

1. I got this idea from the author Neil Strauss. Listen to an interview Tim Ferriss conducted with him. https://tim.blog/2014/06/24/neil-strauss/

34. Timely Questions

1. I highly recommended Douglas Flemons & Leonard Granlik's, 2013 book Relational Suicide Assessment on this topic.

Flemons, D., & Granlnik, L. M. (2013). *Relational suicide assessment: Risks, resources, and possibilities for safety*. New York: W. W. Norton & Company.

35. Timeless Questions

1. This question is adapted from Atul Gwande's 2014 book, Being Mortal.

Gawande, A. (2014). *Being mortal: Medicine and what matters in the end*. New York: Metropolitan Books.

36. Timely and Timeless Questions?

1. The term "Psychache", as first seen in Jon Frederickson's (2017) book, The Lies We Tell Ourselves, is a term used by a suicidologist, Edwin Shneidman. He proposed that suicide is an unbearable psychological pain—hurt, anguish, soreness, and aching.

2. See Friar Richard Rohr's book, Falling Upward.

Rohr, R. (2011). *Falling upward: A Spirituality for the two halves of life*. San Francisco: Jossey-Bass.

3. See a short blogpost I did On Suicide: Do Not Make a Permanent Decision... (https://darylchow.com/fullcircles/2017/10/13/on-suicide-do-not-make-a-permanent-decision/)

37. Healing Questions

1. Anthony Greenwald highlights an important point that people are persuaded by what they tell themselves, rather than the actual content of the message, He called this the "cognitive response model"

Greenwald, A. G. (1968). Cognitive Learning, Cognitive Response to Persuasion, and Attitude Change. *Psychological Foundations of Attitudes* (pp. 147-170): Academic Press.

2. In the tradition of narrative therapy, see Karl Tomm's short article:

Tomm, K. (1989). Externalizing the problem and internalizing personal agency. *Journal of Strategic & Systemic Therapies, 8*(1), 54-59. doi: https://doi.org/10.1521/jsst.1989.8.1.54

3. The interview with Larry King was conducted by author and

journalist Cal Fussman. See https://tim.blog/2017/08/16/larry-king/ The segment cited in this chapter was at 49:00 min.

38. Don't Just Empathise; Say It.

1. Michael Fishman's website: michaelfishmanconsulting.com

39. Call to Action

1. Burns, D. D., & Spangler, D. L. (2000). Does psychotherapy homework lead to improvements in depression in cognitive-behavioral therapy or does improvement lead to increased homework compliance? *Journal of Consulting and Clinical Psychology,* 68(1), 46-56. doi:http://dx.doi.org/10.1037/0022-006X.68.1.46

40. Be a "With-ness"

1. I acknowledge that I must have deviated from the rich and complex meaning of John Shotter's theory of "withness-thinking". Shotter explains "Withness (dialogic)-thinking is a form of reflective interaction that involves coming into living contact with an other's living being, with their utterances, their bodily expressions, their words, their 'works'." (p. 54). See The Short book of Withness-Thinking (John Shotter,2005), http://www.johnshotter.com/wp-content/uploads/2014/10/Shotter-Shortbook-of-Withness.pdf

2. For more about the outcome rating scale, see the Feedback Informed Treatment Manuals: https://scott-d-miller-ph-d.myshopify.com/collections/fit-manuals, or download the following article: https://www.academia.edu/9361951/Feedback_Informed_Treatment_FIT_Achieving_Clinical_Excellen

Miller, S. D., Hubble, M. A., Seidel, J. A., Chow, D., & Bargmann, S. (2014). Feedback Informed Treatment (FIT): Achieving clinical excellence one person at a time. *Independent Practitioner, 34*(3), 78-84.

41. How Do You Close a First Session

1. Redelmeier, D., Katz, J., & Kahneman, D. (2013). Memories Of Colonoscopy: A Randomized Trial. *Pain, 104*, 187-194.

2. Pink, D. H. (2018). *When: The scientific secrets of perfect timing.* Great Britain: Riverhead Books.

3. Over the years, I've had clients who tell me that they've kept some of the key pointers we've written on index cards in their wallets or stuck it to their fridge doors. Over time, I've found the act of either the client or I writing it down on a card for them to keep, has served to punctuate core themes, which in turn, influenced memory recall. These index cards have become slow-and-long-lasting release pills.

42. Don't Just Ask for Feedback, Give Some.

1. In Therapy Forever? Enough Already. The New York Times, by Jonathan Alpert, http://www.nytimes.com/2012/04/22/opinion/sunday/in-therapy-forever-enough-already.html

2. On Being podcast interview with David Whyte, https://onbeing.org/programs/david-whyte-the-conversational-nature-of-reality/

43. Developing a Visual of Client's Outcomes

1. Go to the final chapter of this book, **A Gift For You** to see the instructions of how to download the ORS and SRS Chart and Cheat Sheet.

2. Go to Dr. Scott D Miller's website to download the measures for free: https://scott-d-miller-ph-d.myshopify.com/collections/

performance-metrics/products/performance-metrics-licenses-for-the-ors-and-srs

SECTION III: BUILDING A CULTURE OF LEARNING

44. The Use of Routine Outcome Monitoring (ROM)

1. See the following two studies:

Miller, S. D., Duncan, B. L., Brown, J., Sparks, J., & Claud, D. (2003). The outcome rating scale: A preliminary study of the relia-bility, validity, and feasibility of a brief visual analog measure. *Journal of Brief Therapy*, 2(2), 91-100.

Duncan, B. L., Miller, S. D., Reynolds, L., Sparks, J., Claud, D., Brown, J., & Johnson, L. D. (2003). The session rating scale: Psychometric properties of a "working" alliance scale. *Journal of Brief Therapy*, 3(1), 3-12.

2. I highly recommend you to check out the Feedback Informed Treatment (FIT) manuals for more details on how to use the measures like the ORS and SRS (https://www.centerforclinicalex-cellence.com/store)

3. See the following two studies:

Evans, C., Mellor-Clark, J., Margison, F., & Barkham, M. (2000). CORE: Clinical outcomes in routine evaluation. *Journal of Mental Health*, 9(3).

Evans, C., Connell, J., Barkham, M., Margison, F., McGrath, G., Mellor-Clark, J., & Audin, K. (2002). Towards a standardised brief outcome measure: Psychometric properties and utility of the CORE-OM. *British Journal of Psychiatry*, 180(1), 51-60. doi:http://dx.doi.org/10.1192/bjp.180.1.51

4. In my private practice in Australia, I supplement the use of

CORE-10 at the 1st, 5th and 10th (and every subsequent 5th) session because clients need to revisit their GPs at the 6th session to continue for another 4 sessions. Under the federal Better Access scheme, residents are given rebates for a total of 10 sessions in a calendar year.

5. Chow, D. L. (2011). The right to recovery. In P. Yap, D. L. Chow, S. Lu, & B. Lee (Eds.), *The write to recovery: Personal stories and lessons about recovery from mental health concerns* (pp. 1-19). Singapore: Wellspring Catholic Books.

45. Why Use Formal Feedback?

1. Miller, S. D., Hubble, M. A., Chow, D. L., & Seidel, J. A. (2015). Beyond measures and monitoring: Realizing the potential of feedback-informed treatment. *Psychotherapy, 52*(4), 449-457. doi: http://dx.doi.org/10.1037/pst0000031

2. Duncan, B. L., Miller, S. D., & Sparks, J. A. (2004). *The heroic client: A revolutionary way to improve effectiveness through client-directed, outcome-informed therapy (rev. ed.).* San Francisco, California: Jossey-Bass Inc.

3.Hannan, C., Lambert, M. J., Harmon, C., Nielsen, S. L., Smart, D. W., Shimokawa, K., & Sutton, S. W. (2005). A lab test and algorithms for identifying clients at risk for treatment failure. *Journal of Clinical Psychology, 61*(2), 155-163. doi:10.1002/jclp.20108

4. Wampold, B. E., & Brown, G. S. (2005). Estimating variability in outcomes attributable to therapists: A naturalistic study of outcomes in managed care. *Journal of Consulting & Clinical Psychology, 73*(5), 914-923. doi:10.1002/jclp.20110

5. Seidel, J. A., Miller, S. D., & Chow, D. L. (2014). Effect size calculations for the clinician: Methods and comparability. *Psychotherapy Research, 24*(2), 470-484. doi:10.1080/10503307.2013. 840812

46. Deliberate Practice

1. See pp. 278-279 of Ericsson, K. A., & Lehmann, A. C. (1996). Expert and exceptional performance: Evidence of Maximal Adaptation to Task Constraints. *Annual Review of Psychology, 47*(1), 273-305. doi:10.1146/annurev.psych.47.1.273

2. Here's a list of reference articles on the development of expertise in various professions:

Cote, J., Ericsson, K., & Law, M. P. (2005). Tracing the Development of Athletes Using Retrospective Interview Methods: A Proposed Interview and Validation Procedure for Reported Information. *Journal of Applied Sport Psychology, 17*(1), 1-19. doi:10.1080/10413200590907531

Ericsson, K. A. (2007). An expert-performance perspective of research on medical expertise: the study of clinical performance. *Medical Education, 41*(12), 1124-1130. doi:10.1111/j.1365-2923.2007.02946.x

Ericsson, K. A., Krampe, R. T., & Tesch-Romer, C. (1993). The role of deliberate practice in the acquisition of expert performance. *Psychological Review, 100*(3), 363-406.

Gobet, F., & Charness, N. (2006). Expertise in Chess. In K. A. Ericsson, N. Charness, P. J. Feltovich, & R. R. Hoffman (Eds.), *The cambridge handbook of expertise and expert performance* (pp. 523-538). Cambridge: Cambridge University Press.

Mamede, S., Schmidt, H. G., Rikers, R. M. J. P., Penaforte, J. C., & Coelho-Filho, J. M. (2007). Breaking down automaticity: case ambiguity and the shift to reflective approaches in clinical reasoning. *Medical Education, 41*(12), 1185-1192. doi:10.1111/j.1365-2923.2007.02921.x

Norman, G., Eva, K., Brooks, L., & Hamstra, S. (2006). Expertise in medicine and surgery. In K. A. Ericsson, N. Charness, P. J.

Feltovich, & R. R. Hoffman (Eds.), *The Cambridge handbook of expertise and expert performance* (pp. 339-353). Cambridge: Cambridge University Press.

Rikers, R. M. J. P., & Verkoeijen, P. P. J. L. (2007). Clinical expertise research: a history lesson from those who wrote it. *Medical Education, 41*(12), 1115-1116. doi:10.1111/j.1365-2923.2007.02920.x

Schmidt, H. G., & Rikers, R. M. (2007). How expertise develops in medicine: knowledge encapsulation and illness script formation. *Medical Education, 41*(12), 1133-1139. doi:10.1111/j.1365-2923.2007.02915.x

Sonnentag, S., & Kleine, B. M. (2000). Deliberate practice at work: A study with insurance agents. *Journal of Occupational and Organizational Psychology, 73*(1), 87-102. doi:http://dx.doi.org/10.1348/096317900166895

3. Feltovich, P. J., Prietula, M. J., & Ericsson, K. (2006). Studies of Expertise from Psychological Perspectives. In K. A. Ericsson, N. Charness, P. J. Feltovich, & R. R. Hoffman (Eds.), *The Cambridge handbook of expertise and expert performance* (pp. 41-67). Cambridge: Cambridge University Press.

4. Ericsson, K. A. (2009). Enhancing the development of professional performance: Implications from the study of deliberate practice. In K. A. Ericsson (Ed.), *Development of professional expertise: Toward measurement of expert performance and design of optimal learning environments* (pp. 405-431). New York, NY: Cambridge University Press; US.

5. Chow, D. (2014). *The study of supershrinks: Development and deliberate practices of highly effective psychotherapists.* (PhD), Curtin University, Australia.

Chow, D., Miller, S. D., Seidel, J. A., Kane, R. T., Thornton, J., &

Andrews, W. P. (2015). The role of deliberate practice in the development of highly effective psychotherapists. *Psychotherapy, 52*(3), 337-345. doi: http://dx.doi.org/10.1037/pst0000015

6. See p.425 of Ericsson, K. A. (2009). Enhancing the development of professional performance: Implications from the study of deliberate practice. In K. A. Ericsson (Ed.), *Development of professional expertise: Toward measurement of expert performance and design of optimal learning environments* (pp. 405-431). New York, NY: Cambridge University Press; US.

7. See the following two studies:

Ericsson, K. A., Nandagopal, K., & Roring, R. W. (2009). Toward a science of exceptional achievement: Attaining superior performance through deliberate practice. In W. C. Bushell, E. L. Olivio, & N. D. Theise (Eds.), *Longevity, Regeneration, and Optimal Health: Integrating Eastern and Western Perspectives (Annals of the New York Academy of Sciences)* (pp. 199-217). River Street, Hoboken: Wiley-Blackwell.

Krampe, R., & Ericsson, K. (1996). Maintaining excellence: Deliberate practice and elite performance in young and older pianists. *Journal of Experimental Psychology: General, 125*(4), 331-359.

8. Chow, D. (2017). The practice and the practical: Pushing your clinical performance to the next level. *Prescott, David S [Ed]; Maeschalck, Cynthia L [Ed]; Miller, Scott D [Ed] (2017) Feedback-informed treatment in clinical practice: Reaching for excellence (pp 323-355) x, 368 pp Washington, DC, US: American Psychological Association; US, 323-355.*

47. Individualised Learning Objectives

1. To receive a copy of the Taxonomy of Deliberate Practice Activities (TDPA) Worksheets and more, go to darylchow.com/firstkiss

2. This process can be applied beyond improving your first

sessions. I've talked about this in a chapter of an edited book. Chow, D. (2017). The practice and the practical: Pushing your clinical performance to the next level. *Prescott, David S [Ed]; Maeschalck, Cynthia L [Ed]; Miller, Scott D [Ed] (2017) Feedback-informed treatment in clinical practice: Reaching for excellence (pp 323-355), Washington, DC, US: American Psychological Association; US,* 323-355.

3. Keller, G., & Papason, J. (2013). *The One Thing: The Surprisingly Simple Truth Behind Extraordinary Results* United States: John Murray Press Learning.

48. A Coach

1. Hunt, E. (2006). Expertise, talent, and social encouragement. In K. A. Ericsson, N. Charness, P. J. Feltovich, & R. R. Hoffman (Eds.), *The cambridge handbook of expertise and expert performance* (pp. 31-38). Cambridge: Cambridge University Press.

2. Watkins, C. E. (2010). Psychotherapy Supervision Since 1909: Some Friendly Observations About its First Century. *Journal of Contemporary Psychotherapy,* 1-11. doi:10.1007/s10879-010-9152-2

3. I first heard this terminology used by Michael Stanier-Bungay, in a related podcast interview on his book the Coaching Habit. This book is a useful read.

Bungay-Stanier, M. (2016). *The coaching habit: Say less, ask more & change the way you lead forever.* Toronto, Canada: Box of Crayons Press.

4. Rousmaniere, T. G., Swift, J. K., Babins-Wagner, R., Whipple, J. L., & Berzins, S. (2014). Supervisor variance in psychotherapy outcome in routine practice. *Psychotherapy Research,* 1-10. doi:10.1080/10503307.2014.963730

5. See blogpost from Frontiers of Psychotherapist Development, Develop Fist Principles Before the Methods, http://darylchow.

com/frontiers/2017/10/27/develop-first-principles-before-the-methods/

6. Page 155 of Mckeown, G. (2014). *Essentialism: The disciplined pursuit of less*. Great Britain: Random House Group Company.

7. See page 41 of Wooden, J., & Yaeger, D. (2009). *A game plan for life: The power of mentoring*. New York: Bloomsbury.

49. Feedback

1. See the following exceptions:

Abbass, A. (2004). Small group videotape training for psychotherapy skills development. *Acad Psychiatry, 28*(2), 151-155. doi:10.1037/a0022427

Rousmaniere, T., & Frederickson, J. (2013). Internet-Based One-Way-Mirror Supervision for Advanced Psychotherapy Training. *The Clinical Supervisor, 32*(1), 40-55. doi:10.1080/07325223.2013.778683

2. See p. 422 of Ericsson, K. A. (2009). Enhancing the development of professional performance: Implications from the study of deliberate practice. In K. A. Ericsson (Ed.), *Development of professional expertise: Toward measurement of expert performance and design of optimal learning environments* (pp. 405-431). New York, NY: Cambridge University Press; US.

3. Hattie, J., & Timperley, H. (2007). The power of feedback. *Review of Educational Research, 77*(1), 81-112.

4. One caveat: Your supervisor/coach/mentor must be familiar with this framework, and he or she must be focused on client outcomes. If not, you would end up with quite a bit of struggle trying to integrate routine outcomes monitoring and deliberate practice principles into your professional development.

50. Successive Refinement

1. See the following three studies:

Beutler, L. E., Malik, M., Alimohamed, S., Harwood, T. M., H., T., Noble, S., & al., e. (2004). Therapist Variables. In M. J. Lambert (Ed.), *Bergin and Garfield's handbook of psychotherapy and behavior change* (5th ed., pp. 227-306). New York: Wiley.

Chow, D. (2014). *The study of supershrinks: Development and deliberate practices of highly effective psychotherapists.* (PhD), Curtin University, Australia.

Wampold, B. E., & Brown, G. S. (2005). Estimating variability in outcomes attributable to therapists: A naturalistic study of outcomes in managed care. *Journal of Consulting & Clinical Psychology, 73*(5), 914-923. doi:10.1002/jclp.20110

2. See blogpost, *What Does Deliberate Practice Look Like?*

darylchow.com/frontiers/2018/02/18/what-does-deliberate-practice-look-like/

3. See the following three studies:

Ericsson, A. K. (1996). The acquisition of expert performance: An introduction to some of the issues. In K. A. Ericsson (Ed.), *The road to excellence: The acquisition of expert performance in the arts and sciences, sports, and games* (pp. 1-50). Mahwah, N.J.: Lawrence Erlbaum Associates.

Ericsson, K. A. (2004). Deliberate practice and the acquisition and maintenance of expert performance in medicine and related domains. *Academic Medicine, 79*(10 Suppl). doi:10.1111/j.1553-2712.2008.00227.x.

Ericsson, K. A. (2006). The Influence of experience and deliberate practice on the development of superior expert performance. In K. A. Ericsson, N. Charness, P. J. Feltovich, & R. R. Hoffman (Eds.), *The Cambridge handbook of expertise and expert performance* (pp. 683-703). Cambridge: Cambridge University Press.

51. Performance Feedback Versus Learning Feedback

1. Bjork, E. L., & Bjork, R. A. (2011). Making things hard on yourself, but in a good way: Creating desirable difficulties to enhance learning *Psychology and the real world: Essays illustrating fundamental contributions to society* (pp. 56-64). New York, NY: Worth Publishers; US.

2. See the following three studies:

Beutler, L. E., Malik, M., Alimohamed, S., Harwood, T. M., H., T., Noble, S., & al., e. (2004). Therapist Variables. In M. J. Lambert (Ed.), *Bergin and Garfield's handbook of psychotherapy and behavior change* (5th ed., pp. 227-306). New York: Wiley.

Chow, D. (2014). *The study of supershrinks: Development and deliberate practices of highly effective psychotherapists.* (PhD), Curtin University, Australia.

Ericsson, K. A. (2006). The Influence of experience and deliberate practice on the development of superior expert performance. In K. A. Ericsson, N. Charness, P. J. Feltovich, & R. R. Hoffman (Eds.), *The Cambridge handbook of expertise and expert performance* (pp. 683-703). Cambridge: Cambridge University Press.

3. Shute, V. J. (2008). Focus on formative feedback. *Review of Educational Research,* 78(1), 153-189. doi:http://dx.doi.org/10.3102/0034654307313795

52. Eliciting Client Feedback

1. Duncan, B. L., Miller, S. D., Reynolds, L., Sparks, J., Claud, D., Brown, J., & Johnson, L. D. (2003). The session rating scale: Psychometric properties of a "working" alliance scale. *Journal of Brief Therapy,* 3(1), 3-12.

2.Bordin, E. S. (1979). The generalizability of the psychoanalytic concept of the working alliance. *Psychotherapy: Theory, Research & Practice, 16*(3), 252-260. doi:http://dx.doi.org/10.1037/h0085885

3. Frank, J. D., & Frank, J. B. (1993). *Persuasion and healing: A comparative study of psychotherapy* (3rd ed.). Baltimore: Johns Hopkins University Press.

4. Owen, J., Miller, S. D., Borg, V., Seidel, J. A., & Chow, D. (2016). The alliance in the treatment of military adolescents. *Journal of Consulting & Clinical Psychology*.

5. Chow, D. (2014). *The study of supershrinks: Development and deliberate practices of highly effective psychotherapists.* (PhD), Curtin University, Australia.

6. I highly recommend reading John Brockman's compilation *of leading scientists and thinkers in the Edge book, What Have You Changed Your Mind About?* .

Brockman, J. (Ed.) (2009). *What Have You Changed Your Mind About?: Today's Leading Minds Rethink Everything (Edge Question Series). New York: Harper Collins.*

I wrote a related blog post about this. See: http://darylchow.com/ frontiers/2017/01/21/what-have-you-changed-your-minds-about/

7. The use of a simple two-minute checklist in four major developing world and four developed world hospitals helped to reduce major complications for surgical patients by 36 percent, and more importantly, reduced mortality rates by 47 percent. For more details, see Atul Gwanade's groundbreaking book, The Checklist Manifesto.

Gwanade, A. (2010). *The Checklist manifesto: How to get things right*. Great Britain: Profile Books.

53. Receiving Client Feedback

1. Stone, D., & Heen, S. (2015). *Thanks for the feedback: The science and art of receiving feedback well*. New York: Penguin Random House LLC.

54. Now, Let's Play with Feedback

1. Nissen-Lie, H. A., Monsen, J. T., Ulleberg, P., & Ronnestad, M. H. (2012). Psychotherapists' self-reports of their interpersonal functioning and difficulties in practice as predictors of patient outcome. *Psychotherapy Research*, 1-19. doi:10.1080/10503307.2012.735775

2. Chow, D. (2014). *The study of supershrinks: Development and deliberate practices of highly effective psychotherapists*. (PhD), Curtin University, Australia.

3. See the following articles by Janet Metcalfe and her colleagues:

Barbie, J. H., & Metcalfe, J. (2012). Making related errors facilitates learning, but learners do not know it. *Memory & Cognition, 40*(4), 54-527. doi:10.3758/s13421-011-0167-z

Butterfield, B., & Metcalfe, J. (2001). Errors Committed With High Confidence Are Hypercorrected. *Journal of Experimental Psychology: Learning, Memory, & Cognition November, 27*(6), 1491-1494.

Butterfield, B., & Metcalfe, J. (2006). The correction of errors committed with high confidence. *Metacognition and Learning, 1*(1), 69-84. doi:http://dx.doi.org/10.1007/s11409-006-6894-z

Metcalfe, J., & Finn, B. (2011). People's hypercorrection of high-confidence errors: Did they know it all along? *Journal of Experimental Psychology: Learning, Memory, and Cognition, 37*(2), 437-448. doi:http://dx.doi.org/10.1037/a0021962

55. Recording Your First Sessions

1. Briggie, A. M., Hilsenroth, M. J., Conway, F., Muran, J. C., & M.,

J. J. (2016). Patient comfort with audio or video recording of their psychotherapy sessions: Relation to symptomatology, treatment refusal, duration, and outcome. *Professional Psychology: Research and Practice, 47*(1), 66-76. doi:http://dx.doi.org/10.1037/a0040063

2. See this two-part blogposts on Blackbox Thinking for Psychotherapists:

darylchow.com/frontiers/2018/03/26/blackbox-thinking-for-psychotherapists-part-i-of-ii/

darylchow.com/frontiers/2018/03/31/blackbox-thinking-for-psychotherapists-ii/

56. Why Do We Need To Score Your First Sessions?

1. Duarte, N. (2010). *Resonate: Present visual stories that transform audiences.* New Jersey: John Wiley and Sons.

2. Campbell, J. (1949). *The hero with a thousand faces.* California: Pantheon Books.

3. Stern, D. N. (2010). *Forms of vitality: Exploring dynamic experience in psychology, the Arts, Psychotherapy, and Development.* Oxford: Oxford University Press.

57. How Do We Score a First Session?

1. Suffice to say, seek formal permission from your client to do so. See bonus materials (last chapter: A Gift for You) for a sample template of client consent form for audio/video recording.

2. Empirical validation of the Impact of Session Grid (ISG) needs to be conducted. The current limited evidence is supported by my clinical work and the mentorship I give to clinicians I supervise and consult with. Though I had previously no idea of Shawn Coyne's method of mapping out storytelling, called the Story Grid, there are similarities. Much of my initial thinking about the Impact of Session Grid (ISG) were inspired from Bradford

Keeney's (1990) book " Improvisational Therapy" and Daniel Stern's (2010) Forms of Vitality.

Keeney, B. P. (1991). *Improvisational therapy: A practical guide for creative clinical strategies.* New York, NY: Guilford Press; US.

Stern, D. N. (2010). *Forms of vitality: Exploring dynamic experience in psychology, the Arts, Psychotherapy, and Development.* Oxford: Oxford University Press.

3. Heath, C., & Heath, D. (2017). *The Power of moments: Why certain moments have extraordinary impact.* New York: Simon & Schuster.

58. Figure Out Your Circle of Development

1. On the topic of helping clients and ourselves face reality, I highly recommend Jon Frederickson's book The Lies We Tell Ourselves. Poetically and clearly written, it's also interspersed with useful clinical examples.

Frederickson, J. (2017). *The lies we tell ourselves: How to face the truth, accept yourself, and create a better life.* Kansas City, MO: Seven Leaves Press.

2. Vygotsky, L. S. (1978). *Mind in society: The development of higher psychological processes.* Cambridge, MA: Harvard University Press.

3. Here is a related blogpost I wrote on "When Someone Says "I Lack Discipline":

http://darylchow.com/Daryl_Chow/Blog/wordpress/fullcircles/2017/05/29/when-someone-says-i-lack-the-discipline/

Closing:

1. I first came across this story of "Any Old Map Will Do" in the book Yes to Mess, Frank Barrett 2012 (pp.10-11). I traced the origins, and it's probably first told by Medical researcher Oscar Hechter in 1972. He cited the story to be from Albert Szent-Györ-

gyi. See: http://andrewgelman.com/2012/04/23/any-old-map-will-do-meets-god-is-in-every-leaf-of-every-tree/

2. I wrote a series of blogposts on the topic of developing first principles. Here's are the links to them:

http://darylchow.com/frontiers/2017/10/27/develop-first-principles-before-the-methods/

http://darylchow.com/frontiers/2017/11/06/three-ways-to-develop-first-principles-in-your-clinical-practice

http://darylchow.com/frontiers/2017/11/10/first-principles-the-5-step-process-for-deep-and-accelerated-learning-in-therapy/

9 780648 267010